A Manual for Change

A Manual for Change

Terry Wilson

Gower

Published by
Gower Publishing Limited
Gower House
Croft Road
Aldershot
Hampshire GU11 3HR
England

Gower
Old Post Road
Brookfield
Vermont 05036
USA

Terry Wilson has asserted his right under the Copyright, Designs and Patents Act 1988 to be identified as the author of this work.

British Library Cataloguing in Publication Data

Wilson, Terry
  Manual for Change
  I. Title
  658.4

ISBN 0–566–07460–5

Library of Congress Cataloging-in-Publication Data

Wilson, Terry, 1942–
  A manual for change / Terry Wilson.
      p.   cm.
  Includes index.
  ISBN 0–566–07460–5:
  1. Organizational change–Handbooks, manuals, etc. I. Title.
HD58.8.W553 1994
658.4'08–dc20   93–36858
                                                                                          CIP

Typeset in 12 point Baskerville by Bournemouth Colour Graphics and printed in Great Britain at the University Press, Cambridge.

To Vivien and Nicholas

Contents

List of figures   ix

Preface   xi

Acknowledgements   xv

Using the manual   1

Change programme focus   5
    The scale of change

Change process profile   9
    The twelve factors

Factor one: Perspectives   21
    Maintaining the overall view

Factor two: The change champion   35
    Leading the change

Factor three: The nature of change   47
    Identifying the change affecting us

Factor four: Unified management vision   61
    Importance of management agreement

Factor five: Change of organization philosophy   71
    Modernizing the organization

Factor six: Change phases   85
    Four phases of change

Contents

Factor seven: The 10/90 rule   103
Vision and real change

Factor eight: Transitional management   113
Management role and style

Factor nine: Teamwork   125
Importance of teams

Factor ten: Changing behaviour   135
Identifying the main influences

Factor eleven: Expertise and resources   149
Assessing requirements

Factor twelve: Dangers and pitfalls   161
Planning to avoid difficulties

List of figures

Change process profile   15

2.1 Change champion roles   35

7.1 Energy and commitment profile   104

8.1 Development of managers and teams   114

8.2 Managerial role change   116

8.3 Development of managerial style   118

9.1 The cascade principle   129

10.1 Influences on behaviour   135

Preface

Change can build or destroy organizations. Change can be invisible or blatant. Change can creep forward imperceptibly or advance at hurricane speed. Change may arise from one source or strike from many sources at once. Change can be exhilarating or depressing. Change can dominate or be managed.

For these powerful reasons the study and exploitation of change is a stimulating challenge. At a more pragmatic level, change is affecting and shaping managers' jobs and what they are expected to do hour by hour, day by day, month by month and year by year.

One of the main problems for most managers is that they are not given a handful or a briefcase full of change to deal with in some predetermined way. Many of the tasks in organizations can be completed using known procedures and routines. For example, building an office block, carrying out 50 open-heart surgery operations, sending pay cheques to 20,000 local council workers or constructing 50 motor cars. These tasks are readily identified, with known measurements of either success or failure. The management of change, however, is different. It relies on managers scanning their environment to discover what is happening, making sense of it and finally reacting and taking decisions. Such decisions will be based on an interplay between the environmental activity and the managers' own ideas and thinking. They will therefore be influenced by the managers' values, experiences and prejudices, and open to attack and criticism from others with differing perceptions.

Managing change is therefore a difficult and complex affair. In some organizations change is handled very badly, or not handled at all. Slow organizational decay sets in as the organization holds on to values, ideas, technology, procedures and practices that will eventually cause it to cease operating. Other organizations do achieve change but only when facing a catastrophe and possible destruction. One reason for this is that managers are captives of their past successes and experience. They continue to do what they have done successfully in the past, even though because of changed circumstances they are now doing the wrong things. Organization change should therefore operate as much on the thinking skills of managers as on any other element. This is because it is management thinking and action which ultimately determine an organization's characteristics and the culture in which people work.

This manual is based on my experience of change programmes over the past 15 years, work which continues with several fascinating projects. It has involved working at every level in organizations, with directors and executive boards, research teams, security personnel, accountants, production managers, office staff, personnel and training people, engineers, technicians, operatives, sales staff and trade union committees. The experience has covered many industries from agriculture to paper-making, building products to breweries, food manufacture to tool hire and aeroplane production to consultancy. A number of these assignments lasted for several years. This alone was a unique experience as it enabled me to observe organizations and managers over time as they slowly built their new organizations.

At the same time I was also starting, developing and building several businesses of my own, and was thus having to manage issues similar to those that client organizations were facing. Business acquisition, product development, marketing, selling, cash flow, financial controls, staff motivation, and team building all had to be handled effectively. My businesses experienced the euphoria of growth and development in a booming economy when sometimes we were so busy that we could not take on another project. I also had to deal with the reverse, the economic recession when growth was replaced by contraction and projects and money became increasingly scarce. The excitement and euphoria of growth were replaced by pain and depression as many difficult decisions had to be made and implemented to keep the businesses viable.

I wrote this manual because in my years of consulting I have not discovered any published material that deals comprehensively with the total process of organization change. Owing to its long timescales and complexity, organization change is frequently tackled by managers developing a general vision or direction and then implementing several interlocking, organization-wide projects which may or may not be successful. Their success or otherwise depends on a number of elements including the financial and economic condition of the organization, its commitment to change, the power of the change champion and so on. More important than all of these is an understanding of what organization change entails and what has to be present for it to be successful, together with the ability to conceptualize and understand a total process that has many facets and a timescale of several years.

Another purpose of the manual is to give managers some concepts and ideas that will enable them to stand back from the day-to-day running of the organization. By thinking in unfamiliar ways about familiar things, they will discover new connections and approaches and develop innovative solutions to handling change.

Each section of the manual is based on thinking and ideas which have been used on actual change programmes. As every organization has unique features and characteristics, it is unlikely that all these ideas will be applicable to every kind of organization. However, many of the ideas should be general enough to be modified to fit most organizations.

The manual has been written so that it not only puts forward thoughts, ideas and concepts about change but also allows an individual manager or groups of managers to work systematically through each section. The manual can be used as a complete programme, starting at the beginning and completing it section by section until the end is reached. Alternatively, managers may wish to dip into specific sections to increase their knowledge and understanding in one particular area.

The manual contains many questionnaires, exercises and action plans. These are designed to enable managers to relate what they are reading to their own organizations and situations and therefore make their own change process more effective.

The Change Process Profile will give managers an initial understanding of the 12 factors on which the manual is based. Managers can assess their level of confidence in handling the factors correctly and measure their increased understanding by reassessing confidence levels after working through the sections and noting any change in scoring.

For most organizations change is difficult and complex to manage. This manual is intended to make the task easier.

Terry Wilson

Acknowledgements

My greatest debt of gratitude is to some of the powerful forces that create change, for without the recession of the late 1980s and early 1990s and the downturn in business activity, I would not have had time to compile this manual. I was too busy helping other managers and organizations to change. There is still uncertainty about whom to blame or indeed thank: Margaret Thatcher, John Major, Norman Lamont, Neil Kinnock, or the world economy!

Special acknowledgements are due to the many organizations that I have worked for on change assignments. The experiences I had with them are the basis of this manual. My special thanks also go to the many managers and fellow consultants who have shared such experiences with me.

Technological change has also played a major role in the compiling of this manual. A modern computer package substantially helped in the rearranging of text and drawing graphics. This task was expertly carried out by Amanda who has a special mastery of computers and therefore greatly assisted me at all stages.

TW

Using the manual

The theme of this manual is the introduction and implementation of organization change. It considers specifically aspects of change which relate to management and people and emphasizes those that are most important.

The manual is about evolutionary as opposed to revolutionary changes, changes which have to happen as far as possible with the consent of the workforce and all employees. It addresses itself to established organizations which have had change forced on them or which see the need to operate differently. Such organizations usually wish to keep their identity intact and retain the best of their familiar working procedures, codes and practices, and the skill and knowledge base of their managers and employees.

This being the case, change must inevitably be a phased process involving several stages. Indeed change for most organizations must take this form. Few organizations can have the luxury of a new 'greenfield' site where everything can be designed to fit the very latest technological and managerial thinking. Nor would they welcome an overnight revolution where the existing managerial regime is replaced by one with completely different philosophies and values and people have to change or suffer the consequences.

Both the 'greenfield' site and the revolutionary approach are feasible and well-used change strategies with different and predictable consequences. The 'greenfield' approach can be an ideal of perfect design in which everything fits and is built into the grand plan. However, it can also be very costly and disruptive to the organization's existing business. The overnight revolution based on overt power and repression can be quick and incisive, but if it is to succeed the old managerial clique may have to be removed completely. In addition, ways may have to be found of restoring the organization's unity and morale.

Change is a complex process and although one can discuss pure change strategies, most strategies will encompass elements of many different approaches. In reality, when you are attempting to do things better and differently with timescales of anything up to several years, there are times when issues have to be resolved and it is not possible to gain everyone's support, so decisions are made and implemented without full consensus and

1

agreement. People will be upset, but the business pressures are such that something has to happen if the organization is to achieve its objectives.

The manual also discusses change that is on a large scale and has far-reaching consequences. This involves the reappraisal and re-evaluation of the organization's mission, objectives, philosophies and how it organizes itself to achieve them. Managers are faced with many alternatives, but the key is to develop a collective management view and vision which is clearly described and communicated to the whole organization. This sets the boundaries and guidelines for the shape of the organization and how future business is to be carried out.

The manual is therefore not about the introduction of a single new system or operating method. With fundamental organizational changes there will be many such systems to be introduced in which people have to think, react and behave in quite new and different ways. For the organization, the real challenge will be to design and implement systems and methods of working that fit in with and support the values that form the foundations of the business and hold it together. This is the real key to successful organization change.

Who can use the manual

The manual can be used by anyone who is interested in implementing managerial and organizational change or in the process of change. Particular groups are:

Senior managers responsible for the survival, growth and direction of their organizations. It will help them to clarify their thinking on the process of change, give them new ideas and concepts to work with and focus their thinking on the kind of management style required. Factor twelve – Dangers and pitfalls – will alert them to some of the problems that can delay or jeopardize any change programme.

Trainers who have to design powerful and imaginative interventions, workshops and courses to equip people to understand, support and adopt change. The manual contains material for inputs and lectures, exercises and action planning which can be readily used or adapted. It is ideal for use as a self-study programme for managers, with the trainer acting as a coach and mentor helping the manager to understand and progress through the numerous stages of change.

Junior managers who are involved in change programmes or who wish to understand more about introducing change into organizations. In most change initiatives it is the more junior managers who have to convert the policies and plans developed by senior managers into practical reality. They have to work on a daily basis with the workers, operatives and front-line staff, implementing new approaches and modes of behaviour. Therefore the more they understand the change the easier their job will be.

Students of change who want to know more about the effect of change on an organization and about how managers respond and deal with it. They will gain valuable insights into such important factors as change timescales, management philosophies, strategies, management roles and behaviour and teamwork, all derived from involvement in actual organizational change projects. They will then be able to contrast the ideas gained with those of other writers on the subject.

Ways of using the manual

The manual is designed to help the reader learn about and understand the main factors in an organization change process and then apply the new insights to their own organization. Each factor is a building block of change. The manual can therefore be used in a number of ways. If you are about to embark on a change initiative it can be used as a general framework on which to base your thinking. If you are part way through a change programme you can use the factors in the manual to evaluate your strategy and to ensure that you are giving sufficient attention to all aspects of the change process. Alternatively, if you are planning change initiatives at some stage in the future the manual can be used as reading material to prepare for change.

Change programme focus

Understanding begins with describing

Organizational change takes many forms and has a wide variety of causes. Before embarking on a change programme, or indeed if you are already in the process of change, you must take an overview of the situation. This can be done by looking at the broad parameters of change that have to be considered and managed, which are given below. Complete the questionnaire on pages 7–8 with the help of the notes which follow.

Scale. Indicate here the scope and size of the programme. Is it a pilot study in a section or department? Perhaps you have selected a particular unit, or maybe your plans entail changing the whole organization.

Investment. Change can rarely take place without considerable investment. How you define it in monetary terms will depend on your organization. Is the sum to be spent the annual change budget figure or does it include additional money?

Timescale. How long do you envisage that the total change process will take? Are you including the time spent on research and planning the change programme? How will the end of the programme be determined – when the operation is working to target or when a change of philosophy and culture has taken place?

Changes. Indicate here the nature of the changes that are taking place. These may range from a change in current operating methods through to a complete change of organization philosophy. The approach required and the investment needed will be different for each level of change.

Impetus for change. What are the reasons for embarking on the change programme, since these will to some extent determine its direction and style? Is the change to do with organization survival or development, since the implications of the strategy adopted can be quite different?

Strategy. How would you describe the strategy driving the change process?

Is it, for example, revolutionary in nature, in other words happening to a very short timescale with many casualties? Or does it have a much longer timescale and grow organically with the full support and co-operation of the organization's employees? Perhaps it is neither of these and change is introduced piecemeal or on a project-by-project basis.

At this very early stage of examining change and the change process you should be beginning to formulate a few ideas and frameworks that will help you to think about a change programme. Often when organizations are undergoing radical change, many people can be left in a state of confusion and uncertainty. This is because they do not have access to the information and data on which the change decisions have been made, or the strategic frameworks to categorize and make sense of the information. Having completed this simple questionnaire you should have a few more ways of thinking about organization change.

This theme is developed further when we examine the Change Process Profile in the next section.

Change programme focus questionnaire

Indicate with a cross ☒ in the appropriate box the type of change programme you are following under each heading. Make notes in the section provided to support your answers.

Scale

	Section	Department	Unit	Organization
	❏	❏	❏	❏

Notes:

Investment

	£100,000+	£1m+	£5m+	£20m+
	❏	❏	❏	❏

Notes:

Timescale

	1 year	2 years	5 years	10 years
	❏	❏	❏	❏

Notes:

Changes

Operating methods	Systems and procedures	Structures and organizations	Philosophy
❏	❏	❏	❏

Notes:

Impetus for change

New technology	Changing market-place	Financial pressures	Organization renewal
❏	❏	❏	❏

Notes:

Strategy

Revolution	Piecemeal	Project by project	Organic and integrated
❏	❏	❏	❏

Notes:

Change process profile

It is often the things that we overlook that are most important

Implementing extensive organization change is a long-term and complex project. However, like any complex process it can be broken down into its component factors. The following twelve factors are of special significance for the success of any change programme. Interestingly, they are not the commercial and physical resources that are needed for any successful project. Every project manager knows that projects must have the correct objectives, organization structure, expertise, project teams, targets, timescales, reporting procedures, control systems, finance, communication and management. In this sense all projects are the same, whether the task is to construct 25 miles of motorway or to build a new factory for canning beans. They can all succeed or fail as a result of a problem with any one of the above elements.

Organization change projects differ in that they are also attempting to change the relationship between human beings and physical resources, how they are organized, relate to each other and work in the most effective, productive and satisfying manner. Therefore the change programme is attempting to redesign not only the physical aspects of the business, but also the human systems. This generates an entirely new set of factors which must be taken into account. Some of these can be built into the design at the very beginning of the project, others have to be considered as the change process progresses; indeed, some may be generated by the change process itself. Like most important factors affecting change, they are continually changing and require particular sensitivity on behalf of the change makers. The twelve factors are described below.

Factor one: Perspectives. The perspective is the conscience of the change process. It is a mechanism that the change makers set up to enable them to receive valid feedback on the effects of their change. In their passion for pushing through the programme, they can sometimes overlook or underestimate conditions being created in certain groups of people or parts of the organization which could seriously jeopardize their plans. Therefore, in the design stage they must decide on the steps to be taken to keep in touch with the areas of the business where difficulties could arise. Such mechanisms include an independent consultant, multi-level project teams, managerial/union teams, 'management by wandering around', attitude surveys and regular formal presentations and discussions.

9

Factor two: The change champion. Radical organization change does not occur unless there is a powerful person, or group of people, who are determined, committed and single minded about changing the business. To this end they risk their careers, knowing that success will bring rewards and glory and failure result in ignominy and the certain loss of jobs. Such people possess vision, energy, style, charisma and an overriding desire to win. They are usually superb communicators and gather like-minded people around them who become infected with their missionary zeal.

Factor three: The nature of change. Managers who are implementing organization change programmes must understand the type of change they are dealing with. Change may come from a number of areas. For example, political and economic conditions, market movements, competitor activity, organization philosophies and management theories. In addition managers are being bombarded with a myriad of new ideas and techniques, such as Total Quality Management, customer care, self-managing teams, performance management and team cultures, all of which they must take account of if they are to remain competitive. The change makers must therefore be very clear about the nature of the change affecting them, the philosophies and ideas they are embracing and how they intend to implement them.

Factor four: Unified management vision. Nothing can be more detrimental to a change programme than managers who are not fully agreed about what they are changing and how they intend to achieve it. Disunity can occur in several areas. In the senior management group, there may not be agreement about the changes and management philosophy. Without direction and guidance from the top, more junior management groups develop their own philosophies and initiatives which may be out of step with what is happening at higher levels. Regarding such issues as organization philosophy, business values and organization design, time must be taken to develop a vision of what is being proposed and implemented so that all managers have a clear understanding.

Factor five: Change of organization philosophy. Many change programmes involve a marked shift in the philosophy of how the business is managed and how it treats employees. The key elements in such a change can be flattening organization hierarchies, devolving authority and responsibility, and creating a quality management, self-managing team culture. These changes strike at the very heart of the business and the style of management that has made each individual successful. People have to rethink many of the values and premises on which their career and profession have been based, but, more importantly, they must also modify their style and behaviour. Quality and teamwork can only flourish if people are allowed to take responsibility for their jobs and actions. Organizations must therefore be very clear about how much they are changing their philosophy and style and make plans and take action to ensure that the change happens.

Factor six: Change phases. There are four fundamental phases that the organization and its people have to go through for change to be implemented successfully. These are developing the vision, accepting the vision, understanding the vision and behaving according to the vision. Each follows the other and has related actions and management initiatives that must be carried through. The meaning of each phase will vary at different levels and sections of the organization. There must therefore be a process of explanation and communication so that people can see and understand the reasons for the change and the part that they play. However, the real test for the change initiative will be the last phase. People have to work and behave according to the change objectives and targets and deliver the organization's products and services effectively and economically.

Factor seven: The 10/90 rule. The champion's vision is important for initiating and sustaining the change process, but it is not sufficient by itself to bring about change. For every 10 units of vision, there have to be 90 units of definition, dedication and hard work. Vision can be highly effective, appeal to the emotions and be a guiding light at a time of confusion and uncertainty. Once it is present the real work begins. From the vision, plans have to be made, project leaders appointed, work groups and teams set up, targets set, procedures changed and training courses run. At the same time discussion and debate have to continue, in order to convince the doubters, win over the sceptics, and if necessary get rid of the antagonists. Such a process can last for several years and requires high commitment and energy, dedication, long hours, stamina and hard work, but all change champions and managers must be prepared for it if the change is to succeed. They have to keep the vision alive and the excitement and energy high.

Factor eight: Transitional management. One element frequently overlooked in change programmes is how all managers and team leaders communicate the vision, implement new policies and gradually bring about behaviour changes in themselves and their work teams. As the change process is gradually introduced they have to adopt one of three distinct styles: leader, manager and team member. There is a transition from one to the other as the team learns, is able to organize itself more effectively and is gradually able to take over its own management. In the early stage of change, leadership and visionary skills are necessary. There is then a period of difficulty and confusion when direction and control is required. Eventually, as the new philosophy and working practices are understood and adopted, teams grow in confidence, become more in charge of their own destiny and the manager is able to act as a team member and mentor. Help and training need to be given to managers as the process develops so that they understand what is happening.

Factor nine: Teamwork. Many initiatives use teamwork as a vehicle for designing and introducing change. The team becomes the foundation for operating the new philosophy and attaining business aims. It is a relatively easy matter to put teams together that have the correct blend of technical skills, but far more difficult and challenging to design and develop teams that have the correct blend of team role skills and personalities. The main reason for this is that insufficient thought is given at the design stage of the programme to teamwork and the characteristics of successful teams. In addition, teamwork should be introduced in a cascade, from the top to the bottom of the organization. If teamwork is to be one of the principal features of the new organization, then a great deal of thought and effort needs to be put into it.

Factor ten: Changing behaviour. The aim of all organization change programmes is to change people's behaviour so that they do their job in a different way. The change makers therefore need to answer a number of fundamental questions. For example, 'Are all people capable of change?', 'What is the most effective way of bringing about the change?', 'What organizational barriers have to be removed?', and 'How long does it take to change behaviour?'. To answer these questions, the change makers need a clear understanding of both people and organizations. Both must be tackled at the same time. It is no use embarking on an expensive programme of training and development for all staff if some of the organizational systems and procedures that supported the old behaviour are not changed as well. Realistic timescales must be set: behaviour change takes years rather than months.

Factor eleven: Expertise and resources. Significant change cannot occur without considerable investment in new and additional resources. The resources fall into three main categories. The first one is usually substantial expenditure on new plant, equipment, technology and systems in an attempt to bring the organization to the forefront of technical competence. A second category is buying knowledge, expertise and skills from consultants and contractors who have been involved in other similar projects. The objective is for them to bring their knowledge and skills into the organization, which can then learn and benefit from it. A third category of resources is the temporary staff required while the change process takes place, for jobs ranging from labourers to senior managers. This frequently leads to two separate structures being set up in the organization: one to carry through the change and the other to maintain the organization in its present state. As the change is worked through, they fuse together.

Factor twelve: Dangers and pitfalls. For many organizations, radical change means plunging into the unknown and some daunting obstacles and difficulties are encountered and have to be overcome. Vision and faith provide the main impetus and carry people forward towards the longer-term goal, but the business still has to be run efficiently and achieve its day-to-day targets. Operating according to both long-term and short-term considerations often creates conflict and tension, which frequently arise if a long-term goal is to change the organization's philosophy and culture. There are times when decisions have to be made which are contrary to the long-term goals, but necessary for current commercial reasons. An example of this kind of situation might be a decision to postpone culture change and teambuilding programmes to satisfy budget requirements. In addition, there may also be technological and organizational blockages which are extremely difficult to overcome and can delay the process by some months. Where possible, the change makers should attempt to identify areas of possible danger in advance and think through ways of overcoming them or even preventing them from occurring.

Having read through the twelve factors, you should now be in a position to assess your own change programme in relation to them. Do this by following the instructions for completing the profile on page 14. As you analyse each factor on the profile, complete the summary which starts on page 16. You will find these summaries useful when you consider each of the factors in greater detail later in the manual.

Summary

You have now considered your programme against the twelve factors on the Change Process Profile and expressed your level of confidence from 0% to 100% in how they are being handled and managed. To support your scores on each factor you have made notes which should be referred to as you read that section in the manual. Which factors are uppermost in your mind as you are about to start the next section of the manual?

Change process profile

Completing the profile

You have considered the twelve factors and reflected on their importance to your change programme. Now examine them in more detail. Take each of the factors in turn and ask yourself the following questions:

- Do I fully understand the factor?

- Has sufficient thought been given to it?

- Has it been incorporated in our plans?

- Are the change makers and other managers handling it correctly?

- Do the right people know about it?

When you have reached a conclusion about a factor, turn to page 15 and express your level of confidence on the profile with a score between 0% and 100%. If you score 0% then you are saying that you have no confidence that the particular factor is being handled correctly, or that no attention has been given to it. On the other hand, if you score 100% then you are totally confident that the factor is understood and being handled perfectly. Scores between 0% and 100% represent increasing degrees of confidence.

Mark your position with an ⊠ on each factor line and then connect them to form a profile.

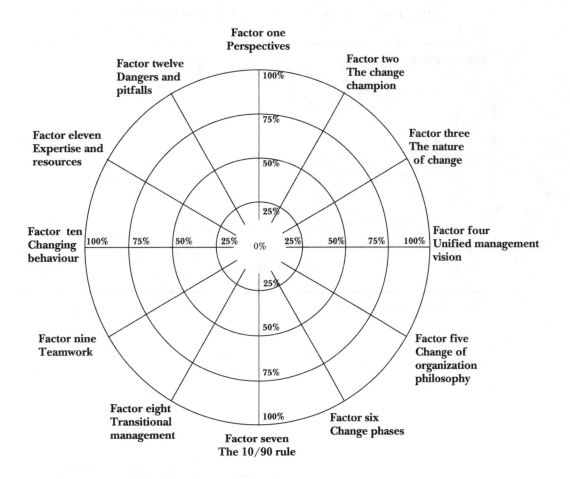

Change process profile

Change process profile

Explanatory notes

Make notes on each factor in the spaces provided below to support your percentage score. Do not at this stage go into too much detail as you will be examining the factors further as you work through the manual. If possible, try to ensure that each factor summary finishes with actions that should be taken.

Perspectives

The change champion

The nature of change

Reproduced from *A Manual for Change*
by Terry Wilson, Gower, Aldershot, 1994.

Unified management vision

Change of organization philosophy

Change phases

The 10/90 rule

Reproduced from *A Manual for Change*
by Terry Wilson, Gower, Aldershot, 1994.

Transitional management

Teamwork

Changing behaviour

Expertise and resources

Dangers and pitfalls

Factor one: Perspectives

Perception is all

Some years ago I visited a director of an organization in Sheffield. On a notice-board in his office he had the phrase 'Perception is All'. In the time that it took to walk across his office, shake hands, pass the normal social pleasantries and then sit down, I decided that I did not understand the message contained in those three words. In fact, driving home after the meeting I came to the conclusion that as well as not understanding the phrase, I also did not believe it to be true. My reason was that it only concentrated on a third of a process. The management process is perceiving, assessing and then making a decision.

However, after further reflection, I began to realize the truth of the phrase. As perception is the first stage of the process, if it is faulty then everything else that follows is also faulty.

The three words give an insight into one of the most important issues in organization change programmes: the different perceptions that people have and how to manage them successfully as part of the change process.

This perspective is even more relevant when one begins to examine the change process in some detail and look at the forces which drive it forward. Behind many change programmes are powerful managers who have a personal mission to succeed and make their mark on the organization. Without such people it is unlikely that radical change would have been attempted in the first place. They often exhibit an all-consuming passion to get their way and pull others along behind them with their enthusiasm and energy. However, once they set a course they are rarely easily diverted.

Frequently an organization does not show the understanding of or commitment to the vision that the change makers would like. The managers leading the change do not understand why everyone cannot see the situation and solutions in the way that they do. In their view, either the organization changes, introduces new products, increases efficiency, cuts overheads, reduces staffing levels, innovates and keeps abreast of competitors, or it goes out of business. The attempt to bridge the gap between the various interest groups and the change makers will take up a good deal of energy and create frustration.

21

We should not be in the least surprised if this kind of problem arises since we see and hear similar conflicts being enacted every time we switch on a television or tune into the radio and listen to political or industrial debates. The politicians and industrialists are going through the same process: that is, people who hold different values and therefore different perceptions of a situation, who then try to convince each other that they are right and the other person is wrong.

Irrespective of the messages conveyed about the potential benefits of any significant change programme, there will inevitably be winners and losers. Some people will do well and others less well. Some people's jobs will be greatly enriched and enhanced with higher status and rewards, others will not be so fortunate and may even be made redundant. The difficulty people face, of course, is that they know exactly what they may lose but are usually unsure of what they may gain. In addition, since they have not experienced the conditions they will face in the future they may not know what to feel about it and may be apprehensive and possibly resistant.

Different levels of people in the organization will have reached different levels of understanding and perception of the changing situation. It is the equivalent of climbing the Eiffel Tower – the higher you climb, the more you see and understand of Paris. You gain by seeing a wider horizon and a broader picture, but you also lose a feeling for life on the streets and in the houses. Balancing these sometimes opposing perceptions is a crucial task for the change makers.

Another interesting point about organizational change is that over time the process itself develops hidden forces that could be damaging. For example, one group of employees in an important strategic position may increasingly feel themselves disadvantaged by the changes. If the correct mechanisms exist for tapping into this growing frustration, then appropriate action can be taken before any damage is done.

All too frequently, case studies of change programmes are published which show an almost clinical, invariably positive history of several years of strategy implementation and the resulting triumphs. However, they take little account of the heart searching which went on, the battles which were fought and the near disasters that occurred. Among all the propaganda, the reality can be overlooked.

Implementing change has always been and will always be a painful process. Some of the pain and difficulty can be avoided if the change makers take more notice of the possible reactions of the potential losers and deal with them early enough, before they cause major disruption.

It is an unfortunate fact of organizational life that the senior managers initiating the change are often blind to the feelings of people at the lower levels of the business. The more junior managers who report to them convey only the good news, which is what they want to hear because it shows them in a favourable light and reinforces the fact that they are doing a competent job. However, the results of such behaviour can be extremely detrimental to the change process in the longer term. Negative attitudes and resistances are built up which should be handled immediately, but are allowed to grow. When they do eventually surface, they can knock the programme off course and set it back months or even years. Therefore to understand and minimize the forces that could be detrimental to the change, a constant sensitivity and check should be built into the process

22

which considers how the change is being perceived.

The methods for achieving this are many and varied, ranging from consultative committees, attitude surveys, project teams and briefing groups to independent consultants. One starting point could be to anticipate the probable areas of difficulty, concern or distress by analysing the winners and losers in the change process. Winning and losing are relative terms, but in any change programme there will be individuals, groups, departments or even entire plants or organizations where the status quo cannot be maintained and which have to be reorganized, redeployed or even made redundant. Taking the issue of redundancy, some people may see themselves as losers if they are made redundant, whereas others may regard themselves as winners, since they can take their severance payment and go and set up the business that they have always dreamed of running.

Winning and losing may also arise through changes in the perceived relative status of different groups of people. This often happens at the middle management levels of an organization if the level of responsibility appears to be being reduced. As operating teams become more self managing, then there is less need for supervisors and middle managers. In a similar vein, as people become more multi-skilled, particularly in a traditional manufacturing environment, then both professionals and craftspeople may feel that they are losing out as some of their skills and hence bargaining power are transferred to others.

Another common area of concern is encountered when organizations decentralize and power, authority, resources and services are transferred to operating units. In this situation there are clear winners and losers as the service functions are diminished and people see their jobs and areas of responsibility either decreasing or increasing.

One event which has a significant effect on people is the introduction of new technology, particularly computer systems. There is hardly an area of an organization that is not affected. We now have systems for receiving visitors in the foyers of organizations where you sign the visitors' book on a computer. Managers send letters and memoranda to each other via electronic mail. Manufacturing and production processes have been streamlined and made more efficient through computer process control and some warehouses are fully automated without the need for any people. When computers are introduced or systems updated, people's jobs can disappear or change dramatically. This either means training for a new occupation, learning new skills or being made redundant.

Your organization

To help you to anticipate and plan for the issues and concerns that will arise during the change process, complete the Perspectives Questionnaire on pages 25–27. This will identify the winners and losers of the change process. Then examine and complete the Perspectives Techniques Survey on pages 28–33. This will help you to decide if you have the correct communication and feedback procedures in operation to handle the change programme. If necessary, refer to the notes that you made on the Change Process Profile on pages 16–19.

Summary

Factor one, Perspectives, helped you to identify some of the issues that may create difficulties during the change programme. It also highlighted the need for effective communication and feedback procedures throughout the organization. You have to decide which are suitable for your organization and which therefore assist the process of change.

Refer to the Change Process Profile on page 15. Now that you have explored and analysed perspectives in greater detail do you want to change your percentage confidence score ?

Perspectives questionnaire

Completing the questionnaire

Consider your change programme. Obviously you will only be able to answer the following questions based on your knowledge of your organization and the changes that will take place. Answer the questions below, analysing both the winners' perception, those who will gain from the change, and the losers' perception, those who will lose from the change.

Who will perceive themselves as winners or losers in the change process?

Winners: .

Losers:

Why are we carrying out the change?

Winners:

Losers:

Reproduced from *A Manual for Change*
by Terry Wilson, Gower, Aldershot, 1994.

What are the main elements to change?

Winners:

Losers:

What will be the key issues in the change process?

Winners:

Losers:

Who will be the key people to implement the change?

Winners:

Losers:

What will be the key measures of success?

Winners:

Losers:

What steps should be taken to ensure that everyone perceives themselves as winners?

Reproduced from *A Manual for Change*
by Terry Wilson, Gower, Aldershot, 1994.

Perspectives techniques survey

Completing the survey

To ensure that you maintain a valid perspective on the change programme, you need to set up mechanisms for both communication and feedback in the relevant parts of the organization. Some of these mechanisms may have as prime functions the development and implementation of the change process. Furthermore, it is likely that several will be established techniques, mechanisms or institutions that will be incorporating the change programme as part of their function.

Consider each of the methods below and decide which could be suitable for your change programme. Having decided then describe in detail how you would use the method, how often you would use it, the people involved and who would take the lead in introducing and using the method. Write in the spaces provided below.

Add any other methods that you think are suitable for your change programme.

Method	How to use it	People involved	Leader
Newsletter Regular update on the change programme circulated to all employees.			

Method	How to use it	People involved	Leader
Attitude surveys Structured interviews and questionnaires to a representative sample of employees.			
Management by wandering around Management policy to walk around the organization regularly and seek employees' views on the change programme.			
Consultants Organization employs outside consultants to provide an objective outside view.			
Briefing sheets Regular summaries produced by change makers for managers to brief their teams.			

Reproduced from *A Manual for Change* by Terry Wilson, Gower, Aldershot, 1994.

Method	How to use it	People involved	Leader
Joint project groups Management/union/ employee groups to implement parts of the change programme.			
Steering committee Selected management/ union/employee committee to oversee the change programme.			
Video Make and show a video film on the progress towards change to all employees every six months.			
Roadshows Structured presentation by senior managers to all employees every six months.			

Reproduced from *A Manual for Change* by Terry Wilson, Gower, Aldershot, 1994.

Method	How to use it	People involved	Leader
Change centre Construct a centre to house the change project team. Display progress charts and allow free access to all employees.			
Publications Publish discussion booklets on the main elements of the change process.			
Consultative committee Managers consult with employee representatives on change plans and progress.			
Progress charts Project progress charts circulated to employees.			

Method	How to use it	People involved	Leader
Policy groups Management/employee representatives develop aspects of change policy.			
Poster campaign Posters displayed on notice-boards informing staff of progress.			
Memory cards Plastic cards highlighting aspects of the change programme issued to employees.			
Other			

Method	How to use it	People involved	Leader
Other			
Other			
Other			
Other			

Factor two:
The change champion

Without a champion there is no change

Strategic, systematic and planned change does not occur without the backing and full involvement of a champion. A champion is the person selected, appointed or self-nominated to lead the change programme. From the very beginning it is important to understand the role that the champion will play and the style to be adopted to achieve the change objectives. These will be determined by a) the present state of the organization and b) the mode of change perceived as relevant.

Figure 2.1 shows that determining whether the organization is healthy or unhealthy and deciding which mode of change to adopt result in four change champion roles, one in each quandrant of the matrix.

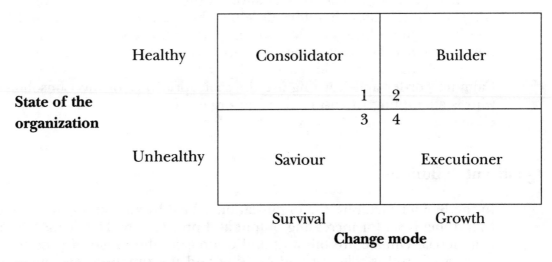

Figure 2.1   Change champion roles

35

State of the organization

This axis measures the current health of the organization in relation to its internal structures and its trading position in the market-place. A healthy organization has modern and relevant products or services that customers want and which satisfy their needs. It has the correct philosophy, managers, organization and procedures to make it efficient, profitable and responsive. In an unhealthy organization the opposite applies. It is out of touch with the market-place or badly organised and unable to compete. Profitability is low, resulting in poor product innovation, lack of investment, inadequate output and low morale.

Change mode

Most organizations embark on a strategy for growth involving increased output, turnover and profitability. Few are content to stand still since this does little to satisfy shareholders' expectations. Furthermore, attempting to stand still often involves slipping back as competitors increase their business. The alternative to the strategy for growth is the strategy for survival. Many organizations in our increasingly competitive world are in danger of going out of business sooner or later unless they change. Their managers therefore plan changes to preserve the organization in its present form.

Quadrant 1: Consolidator

In the Consolidator quadrant the organization is deemed to be healthy, possibly after a period of rapid change or expansion, and it is the objective of the change champion to help it to survive in its present form. Growth is not envisaged, but rather consolidation of the changes already implemented. The Consolidator therefore develops the management teams and how they are organized, reviews the most important aspects of the business and quietly nudges each component into its correct place. The organization is quiet and busy as people learn and practise their new roles and skills. Calmness, order and learning are the main priorities of the Consolidator, who is attempting to ensure that the organization performs at maximum efficiency.

Quadrant 2: Builder

In the Builder quadrant the organization is healthy and aiming for growth. Everything is set for increasing output and profitability. The economic and commercial climate are buoyant and optimistic, the range of products or services offered is relevant and exciting and the organization's morale is high in anticipation of good times ahead. The Builder change champion therefore has to harness, motivate and lead the organization on its path of growth and achievement.

Quadrant 3: Saviour

In the Saviour quadrant the organization is unhealthy and struggling for survival. Unless drastic steps are taken very quickly, bankruptcy is possible. Cash is short, morale is low, there are insufficient orders, standards are poor and despondency pervades the organization. This situation requires the Saviour change champion to have the vision, energy and skill to determine precisely the reason for the organization's problems and set it on a path to recovery. The Saviour is seen as the only person capable of finding a way forward. Everyone knows that the solution could be drastic, but unless such steps are taken the organization will disintegrate.

Quadrant 4: Executioner

In the Executioner quadrant the organization is in an unhealthy state and incapable of performing efficiently, yet it has embarked on a potentially disastrous growth strategy. The managers have either totally misjudged the situation or have been foolhardy. The organization is incapable of fulfilling its obligations to its customers for quality, time or cost, but the managers still press ahead hoping that in the end everything will work out. It is therefore the job of the Executioner change champion to take stock of the situation rapidly and make drastic changes. These may be painful and far reaching, particularly if people will not accept that their existing route is only leading to heavy losses and possible ruin.

The champion's emergence

All organizations are undergoing a degree of change all the time as part of the normal management process. Champions emerge when significant change initiatives are planned that could radically alter the way the organization operates. There is a correlation between the background, experience and qualities of the champion and the nature of the main cause of the change. Causes of change programmes include:

National economic conditions. In times of low interest rates, buoyant trading positions, good business margins, profitability and confidence, organizations embark on a wide variety of change programmes designed to develop the business. In bad times the result can be the opposite, budgets are cut and retrenchment programmes take place.

Political values. Managers may change the way their organizations are designed and run as a direct consequence of the political values espoused by the Government of the day. For example, values of individuality, entrepreneurship, self-sufficiency and share ownership can be built into an organization's operating methods. The results could be people who have self-employed status within the business, payment by results rather than salaries, or less management controls and systems.

Market-place changes. In the ever-changing market-place, an organization's products and services can quickly become out of date. Developing and updating products and adopting new production and management systems can result in enormous organization change.

Management philosophy. Universities, business schools and management theorists are constantly developing different approaches to running and managing organizations. If a business decides to adopt a new management philosophy, this can have a profound effect on the way it operates. Some current management thinking requires that organizations do almost the opposite of what they are now doing: rather than exercising control over their employees, they should give them freedom. Management hierarchies and the management function are cut to a minimum and responsibility for quality lies with each person rather than the quality control function.

New technology. It is almost impossible for organizations to keep up to date with technology. By the time plant, equipment and systems are installed they are out of date. Furthermore, the introduction of computer systems and process-controlled plant can have enormous effects on a business, the way it is managed and its people. New technology can eliminate the need for entire business functions, whole departments and many employees.

Legislation. New laws passed can affect organizations and the way that they operate. There is hardly any aspect of an organization's operation that is not within the domain of some law, regulation or code of practice. If any of these are changed radically then the organization will have to react and reorganize itself. Some legislation can hit at the very heart of a business's trading position, such as a Monopolies and Mergers Commission report or new regulations on product safety. Government legislation can open up or close down entire markets and the organization must remain responsive to its effects.

Quality and standards. Enhanced quality and standards should be objectives of every organization, but they cannot be achieved without considerable management effort and initiative. Often this can lead to a new way of running the business and harnessing the talents and abilities of all employees.

These causes give rise to a general state of dissatisfaction among some or all senior managers about the way the business is operating and the decision is made to take some action. The first step is to appoint someone to lead the change programme, who can come from one of a number of sources:

Appointed from outside the organization. The decision may be made that none of the existing managers has the skills, qualities, background or characteristics required to initiate or lead the change and therefore an external person is appointed. This person then has to understand the business, diagnose its strengths and weaknesses, build a team of like-minded people and formulate plans for change. The advantage of an outside person is that he or she is able to bring fresh thinking and ideas into the business and has experience of operating differently in other organizations. The outsider should also be very clear about what is required in the future, but may not have a complete understanding of the business, its products, operations, customers and history. Furthermore, the person quickly has to establish competence and credibility with the management team, otherwise full assistance and co-operation may not be forthcoming.

Appointed from within the organization. This form of change champion has been assessed by senior managers as having the right qualities to lead the change programme that they envisage. He or she may not currently be in a suitable position to lead such an initiative, but changes can be made to the existing management structure to produce the status, power and influence to perform the task. Unlike someone appointed from outside the business, an insider is likely to know the business, which is a positive advantage. However, this asset can also be a liability since existing business philosophy, values and practices can constrain thinking. The resulting change may not be as innovative and far reaching as it should be for the good of the organization.

Emerge from within the organization. In some organizations there are senior managers who have alternative models of how the business should be run which are far reaching and innovatory. For some reason, either because the conditions are not right or they are not high enough in the management hierarchy to be influential, these people lie dormant. If such a person becomes chief executive and there is at the same time a need for change, a visionary and radical change champion can emerge who can transform the organization. The champion has the benefit of intimate knowledge of the business. In addition, he or she has a well-developed set of philosophies and values around which to design the organization and the way that it produces its goods or services. These have been built up over many years, often through a study of management theories and the practices of other organizations.

If change programmes are to succeed they therefore need a person who can lead and champion the process. However, not every manager has the characteristics to be able to take on such a task. Some attributes which can be observed in successful change champions are:

Vision. Champions leading large-scale organizational change programmes must possess vision in abundance. They have to visualize the shape, style and philosophy of the organization they are building, which will frequently involve overturning many existing practices and ways of doing things. The vision has to be well argued, in written form and seen to be possible and practical.

Clear values. Any new organization design has to be based on the values and beliefs of the change champion. These will determine how business is conducted and how people are treated and motivated to work effectively. Organizations are the direct reflection of the people who manage them. The vision developed for the future state of the business will encapsulate the champion's values. If these values are clear and explicit then the vision and motivation of the change champion will also be well understood. The values can then serve as guidelines for policy and action.

Energy and stamina. Change programmes involve two roles for the change champion: sustaining the output and productivity of the existing organization, and formulating a design for the future. Large-scale change projects often take several years and the workload and pressures on the champion can be enormous, therefore he or she has to be tough and both physically and mentally resilient. In addition, the change may involve entering uncharted territory where there is a great deal of risk and uncertainty, which further increases the need for the champion to have a strong constitution.

Charisma. The champion must have the presence and style to convince everyone of the value and benefits of the change programme. He or she has to be a missionary, conveying the vision, belief, energy and enthusiasm in order to gain followers and support. In the early stages of any change project there is often uncertainty and doubt, which may lead to evidence and data that is given in support of the programme being disputed. Therefore people's commitment must be based on faith in the message of the charismatic champion.

Team builder. Large and complex change programmes cannot be accomplished by one person alone. The champion has to build a team of like-minded managers who also fully support the values, vision and direction of the change and who then become missionaries. This team of managers will also be designers and leaders of the numerous projects that will have to be implemented as part of the programme.

Communicator. The change champion has to be an excellent communicator in almost every medium. Effective communication is an important facet of change and it has to be accomplished at every opportunity with consistency and fervour. Methods that can be used to spread the vision, keep people informed and let them enter the discussions and debates include newsletters, information sheets, large and small group meetings and one-to-one discussions. During times of uncertainty as much communication as possible is required, and the champion must be highly competent and effective at this key skill.

Persuader. People do not abandon long-held beliefs and working practices without a great deal of discussion and persuasion. It is often one of the main objectives of change programmes to convince people in this way. The champion should be a skilled persuader who can project the image of the future organization and then discuss and argue the reasons for moving down that particular route. The opinion formers of the organization in particular must be persuaded of the benefits of the change. These people may be other managers, union representatives, or key groups of employees.

Innovator. Successful organization change requires a great deal of innovative thinking and the change champion has to be the focus for this. The process of innovation should start at the very beginning of the project. The initial ideas and designs have to be forward looking and far reaching enough to ensure that the organization is changed so that it is viable and capable of growing and developing. Furthermore, what is proposed should be seen as different and exciting so that people are attracted to it and want to be part of it. As the changes are proposed and implemented, then new ideas and innovations are required from all project teams and individuals.

Achiever. The change champion has to be a superb achiever and this spirit of achievement and accomplishment has also to be instilled in every person involved in the change process. Organization change programmes comprise a series of interlocking and interdependent projects. A delay on one project can affect all the others, so it is important that deadlines and completion dates are met. In addition, a focus on achievement is vital for the success of the future organization. Teams and individuals therefore need to be imbued with a need for achievement. During the implementation of the programme the champion is in an ideal position to demonstrate his or her own achievement and so set the climate for the future.

Delegator. Organization change programmes are complicated projects and no one person is able to do everything. The champion therefore has to place a considerable amount of faith and trust in managers and project leaders. This trust and delegation of work has to pervade the organization so that authority and responsibility are pushed down as low as possible. Delegation enables all individuals to be part of the change process and encourages innovation. It also sets the style for the new way of managing the organization.

Your organization

Now that you have read about the role, purpose and attitudes of the change champion, consider your own champion by completing the Change Champion Questionnaire on pages 42–43. Having done this, complete the Change Champion Action Plan on pages 44–45. This will give you an overview of your change champion and enable you to plan any improvements that may be necessary. You should refer to the notes that you made on the change champion in Change Process Profile on page 16.

Summary

Factor two, the change champion, stressed the importance of a champion in initiating large-scale organization change. You have assessed the role and attributes of your champion and planned action to help the champion to be even more effective. You should particularly be planning action to ensure that many other change champions are developed in the organization. They then become champions of the new vision and assist in its development and growth.

Refer to the Change Process Profile on page 15 and if necessary change your percentage confidence score in the light of the new insights you have gained about the change champion.

Change champion questionnaire

Completing the questionnaire

Answer the following questions about your change champion.

---

1. Is there an identifiable change champion for the programme who fully recognizes the role and its importance? Put a cross ☒ in the appropriate box.

No	Possibly	Yes
❏	❏	❏

---

2. The change champion and programme leader is

    Name.................................... Position.....................................

    Notes:

---

3. What is the role of the change champion? Put a cross ☒ in the appropriate box.

    Consolidator ❏   ❏ Builder

    Saviour ❏   ❏ Executioner

    Notes:

4. The six main business values of the change champion are:

    1 ....

    2 ....

    3 ....

    4 ....

    5 ....

    6 ....

5. The change champion's rating on the following key attributes are:

	Low								High
	1	2	3	4	5	6	7	8	9

Vision

1	2	3	4	5	6	7	8	9

Clear values

1	2	3	4	5	6	7	8	9

Energy and stamina

1	2	3	4	5	6	7	8	9

Charisma

1	2	3	4	5	6	7	8	9

Team builder

1	2	3	4	5	6	7	8	9

Communicator

1	2	3	4	5	6	7	8	9

Persuader

1	2	3	4	5	6	7	8	9

Innovator

1	2	3	4	5	6	7	8	9

Achiever

1	2	3	4	5	6	7	8	9

Delegator

1	2	3	4	5	6	7	8	9

Reproduced from *A Manual for Change*
by Terry Wilson, Gower, Aldershot, 1994.

Change champion action plan

Completing the action plan

Having worked through this section you will now be much clearer about the importance of the change champion. Reflect on what you have learnt and what is happening in your organization, then complete the following sections.

---

1. Are the value and importance of the change champion recognized in your organization? Specify any action that you feel needs to be taken.

---

2. Is there an understanding of the main business values held by the change champion? Are these values the foundation of the change programme? Specify any action that you feel needs to be taken in this area.

3. Having reviewed the change champion's attributes, specify any action that needs to be taken to make the champion even more effective.

4. Describe the action that should be taken to produce change champions at every level in the organization.

Factor three:
The nature of change

Change is sometimes difficult to perceive but it can be devastating in its effects

Every business and every manager today is surrounded by change. The more fully they can understand and control it, the greater success they will have in managing both themselves and their organization. Some of the aspects of change that have to be understood are described below.

Change is universal

Change pervades all spheres of human activity and there is almost no aspect of commercial or business life that is not affected by change. The environments in which organizations operate are extremely turbulent. Political values and policies change, not only from one government to the next but also from one head of government to another. The economy and trading conditions are in a constant state of flux, at times almost changing from week to week.

Consumer and customer attitudes have undergone dramatic changes which organizations ignore at their peril. Customers have become more aware and are demanding excellence and high service standards. Organizations that do not comply with the desires of their customers will find that they lose business to competitors and for many organizations competition has never been so fierce. New products are developed and rapidly brought to the market-place and marketing and advertising are targeted at the customer. Any organization not operating in this way will soon be overtaken by its competitors. Modern technology and computer systems are developing at an unprecedented rate and affect every part of business life, from how the product is manufactured to the way the manager manages. Organizations have to adopt this new technology since without it they will have a short life. Almost everywhere one looks in organizations significant change is to be found which has to be accommodated and managed.

47

Change is happening more quickly

Not only is change universal but it is also coming about at a faster rate than ever before. The time that products take to develop from conception to reaching the market-place has been drastically reduced in the past few decades. Organizations have therefore had to respond by cutting research, development and production times so that they are in a position to lead rather than follow. Advanced technology and computer systems have contributed to the speed of change. Information can be processed and tasks completed in a fraction of the time required only a decade ago. Similarly, new technology has enabled us to achieve complex tasks that were previously impossible. There is also a freer flow of information, not only between individuals and organizations but across continents. Changes occurring in almost any area of human enterprise can quickly be communicated to others, acting as a stimulus for further activity and change.

Change therefore has a self-generating impetus, since the more there is the more there will be. This idea is written into the philosophies of organizations under such headings as continuous, perpetual or habitual improvement. People and the markets that their organizations serve want to overturn the familiar and seek new approaches to their jobs and the way they run their business. As with most other factors in a competitive society, being first is important for success. This means doing things before other people and hence inexorably speeds up the rate of change.

Change can be invisible

Not all change affecting organizations is readily visible to those who manage the business. There are a number of reasons for this. Managers have to develop a sensitivity to their operating environment and markets. It is easy to be preoccupied with the day-to-day activities of running an organization and not to be able to identify the subtle changes that are taking place until it is perhaps too late and an effective response is no longer possible.

Some changes are imperceptible even to the skilled manager, who may not have experienced such a situation before or who may not see the change as significant. For example, an organization selling leisure and entertainment products to young people which is seeing a reduction in business may not associate the growth in adventure evenings and war games with their own problems.

One of the contributors to invisibility is managers who deny the effect of changes in order to protect their own egos. The change may be too disruptive for them to contemplate or may be against all their beliefs so that they ignore it.

Change is a process

Many changes affecting organizations are part of a process with many facets and a fairly long timescale. Firstly managers need to identify the change processes which will affect their organizations. When this has been done, they should decide if they are prepared to invest time, effort and resources in the change process. The stage at which they decide to invest in the process can be important. One process affecting all organizations was the introduction of the personal computer and computer systems. With hindsight, computers can be seen to have been immeasurably advantageous to organizations – but how would most managers have viewed them in the 1970s? Would they have opted to introduce them?

Other observable change processes to which organizations have had to respond include the movement to low fat food products, the commercialization of public utilities, the increase in worker share ownership and participation, the growth of out-of-town supermarkets, the introduction of cable and satellite television, and so on. Each of these developments will have considerable effects on some organizations. If the process is managed correctly then the organization can be transformed; on the other hand, if the process is neglected or handled badly then it could spell the end of the organization. Therefore it is vital for managers of organizations affected by such long-term change processes to select, plan and monitor their path through the change carefully if they are to remain productive and viable in the future.

Paradigm shifts

Change processes can happen more quickly and have greater effects on some organizations than on others. Such change can be so profound that it completely overturns the very foundations on which an organization or industry was built. The consequent paradigm shift results in a whole set of values, beliefs and ways of thinking being abandoned and replaced with a new set which can be almost the opposite of those previously held. Often paradigm shifts occur when a leap forward is made in some area of human knowledge or technology.

There are many examples of such shifts when what was in place before almost counts for nothing and is destroyed as the new ideas and technology take over. For example, the invention of both the motor car and the aeroplane totally transformed how people thought about travel. In so doing they overtook existing travel technology and business and replaced them with something dramatically different.

The invention of the quartz watch is also an example of a paradigm shift. Until it happened, watch making was based on the engineering crafts of gears, springs and sprockets. After the shift these were replaced by electronics, pulsating crystals and batteries. The Swiss watch industry was unwilling or unable to accommodate the change and as a result was largely destroyed.

It is therefore important for change makers to evaluate the change affecting their organizations. Is it a slow, evolutionary process which can be gradually accommodated, or is it something more profound, a paradigm shift owing to which more drastic action will have to be taken?

Organizations and change

Change must be considered by managers at two levels. The first level is profound, far reaching, global, and large scale, resulting from changes in political systems, economic policies or technological innovation. At this level of change most organizations, except the very large or influential, can only react, make adjustments and seek opportunities for development.

The second level of change is that initiated by the organization itself. From its analysis of its markets and environment, the organization decides which new products, services or systems it should introduce and how best to organize itself to achieve its aims. This causes two activities to take place in the organization at the same time. One is to maintain the existing production flow, while the other is to introduce new ideas, innovate and work differently and better. It is important for the correct balance to be struck between these two activities. Not enough change will result in stagnation, while too much can bring about pressure and frustration at hurried and uncompleted tasks.

All managers should therefore be aware of these aspects of change and attempt to keep them in perspective when they structure their jobs.

People make change successful

Many change programmes greatly underestimate the effect that change will have on people and also how important people are to the success of the change. People have been described as an organization's most valuable and variable asset: valuable in the sense that without people to run them, organizations would not exist; variable in that they can be moved around, transferred to other jobs, promoted, dismissed or made redundant.

No matter how much money is spent on new technology or machinery, change programmes can only be successful if they are able to tap into the energy, commitment and enterprise of people. This is what gives the competitive advantage in the long run. However, few organizations are overflowing with young, enthusiastic people willing to accept new ideas and innovate at the whim of the change makers. There will be groups who fear change, those who see their status and responsibilities diminishing, and organized groups who are hostile and resistant to change. Special attempts will have to be made to develop such people and help them to see the benefits of the change. This is not always an easy task and the patience of the change champions will be frequently tested. It is, however, part of the process of change and must be allowed for in any implementation strategy.

Change builds and destroys

An intriguing question for any manager in an organization undergoing change is whether it will flourish and grow or diminish, wither and eventually die. Even passive observers of organizations cannot fail to notice the phenomenal growth of businesses in such areas as computers, television, newspapers, motor cars, retailing and so on after they have successfully embraced change. Similarly, there are some organizations and even entire industries which have been served badly by change and which have been contracting and struggling to survive for many years. Other organizations have been less fortunate and disappeared almost overnight.

Some of these successes and failures are almost certainly due to large-scale market changes which are difficult to avoid even for the best managed organizations. There are nevertheless many cases of organizations which have been successful in spite of declining markets or depressed trading conditions. These are the ones who have found their niche, organized themselves correctly and responded effectively to change.

Your organization

Those who manage organizations must understand and assess how change will affect them. What may be beneficial to one organization may be detrimental to another. For this reason the different change influences have to be analysed carefully. You can do this for your organization by completing the Nature of Change Questionnaire which starts on page 52. Follow the instructions given and if necessary refer to the notes that you made on the Change Process Profile on pages 16–19.

Summary

Factor three, The nature of change, enabled you to explore some of the components of change and examine the impact of change on your organization. You have also identified the six most significant sources of change, assessed their effects on your organization and specified actions that need to be taken.

Refer to the Change Process Profile on page 15. Consider your percentage confidence score. If necessary adjust it now that you have carefully analysed the changes that are affecting your organization.

Nature of change questionnaire

Completing the questionnaire

This questionnaire is designed to help you think about change as it affects your organization. Complete the following sections to give you a better understanding of change.

---

1. What would happen to your organization if no significant change initiatives were undertaken over the next five years? Answer this question based on your knowledge of the organization and in as much detail as possible.

2. Over the next five years, what will be the sources of change that will affect your organization to a significant extent? Add any others that you feel are relevant and then rank them in order of importance, 1, 2, 3 and so on.

Source of change	Ranking
Increased or decreased market share	
More or less competitor activity	
New legislation	
Political initiatives	
Increased or decreased product range	
The economic situation	
Consumer pressure	
Push for greater profitability	
Improved quality and service	
New regulations	
Organization changes	
Management initiatives	
New technology	
Efficiency and cost cutting	
Environmental issues	
World political conditions	
Supplier activity	
Energy conservation	
Buyer pressure	

Reproduced from *A Manual for Change*
by Terry Wilson, Gower, Aldershot, 1994.

3. Now take the top six sources of change and examine them in more detail by completing the sections below.

Source 1 ....

Describe the source.

What effect will it have on the organization?

How long can we ignore the source before it starts having a detrimental effect on the organization?

What action should be taken?

Source 2..

Describe the source.

What effect will it have on the organization?

How long can we ignore the source before it starts having a detrimental effect on the organization?

What action should be taken?

Source 3 ....

Describe the source.

What effect will it have on the organization?

How long can we ignore the source before it starts having a detrimental effect on the organization?

What action should be taken?

Source 4..

Describe the source.

What effect will it have on the organization?

How long can we ignore the source before it starts having a detrimental effect on the organization?

What action should be taken?

Source 5...

Describe the source.

What effect will it have on the organization?

How long can we ignore the source before it starts having a detrimental effect on the organization?

What action should be taken?

Source 6..

Describe the source.

What effect will it have on the organization?

How long can we ignore the source before it starts having a detrimental effect on the organization?

What action should be taken?

Factor four:
Unified management vision

Changing to a new order is a difficult and precarious task but without unity it is almost impossible

A unified management vision exists when all senior managers share and support the same ideals and future business philosophy as the change champion.

Without management unity, implementing fundamental change can be very difficult if not impossible. Irrespective of the charisma, power and energy of the change champion, it is rarely possible to carry through the programme alone. The task is too complex and too big. The champion has to have dedicated and committed followers who share the vision, are able to articulate it and spread it to other managers and the rest of the organization. It is these managers who will eventually bring about change by leading many of the project teams.

A unified vision also serves as a foundation for management decision making and action. When moving into unknown and untested areas where managers cannot rely on their past experience for support, the philosophy, values and models articulated in the vision can be of immense help. They become the anchors and reference points for action and provide a sense of security. For example, if individual freedom and personal responsibility were the aims of a new management style then this would set the framework for the way teams and subordinates were managed, without the necessity of referring to procedures or manuals. Obviously, any decision to delegate would be based on the manager's assessment of the team's or individual's skill and competence to handle the task delegated and have regard to any formal regulations or safe working procedures.

Another important function of a unified management vision is that it creates energy and enthusiasm within the organization for the change programme. People become interested and excited about the prospect of the management team transforming the organization and in the process making their jobs more satisfying and worthwhile. Obviously not everyone will take this view, as there are some who will see themselves as losers either because of redundancy or changes in jobs or responsibilities. As the change process continues, even these people can become enthusiastic about their future if they are given sufficient help and support. For many people, being made redundant will enable them to move into other areas of interest and benefit them financially. Much depends on the way managers communicate the change to the organization and the help and support they give to those who are displaced.

A unified management vision also gives the organization and people precise goals to aim for. It allows a clear direction to be set with objectives and timescales for the many projects that comprise the programme. The progress of the project must be communicated effectively to the organization in a visible, regular and meaningful way through a variety of media such as discussions, newsletters and meetings. Particularly useful are photographs and video recordings of significant stages in a project, such as the completion of the new restaurant or warehouse facility.

Another important function of a unified management vision is that it reduces uncertainty. One of the most difficult and stressful states for individuals to be in is that of uncertainty. Some people may not like what will be happening to them and their organization, but at least if they are clear about it then they can accommodate it psychologically and adapt to their new future.

Reasons for lack of unity

There are many reasons why a management team may not display unity about a change programme. Some of the most significant and relevant reasons are discussed below.

No change champion. The champion plays an important role in the change process, especially in the vision-building stages. He or she either sets the new philosophy and values of the organization or acts as the catalyst for the management team to develop them. If this role is not carried out effectively then there is a danger that no consistent view will develop and the lack of unity and a distorted message will be communicated to the rest of the organization.

No concept of organization design. Not all managers are able to think about the organization as a whole and design it in the same way as an architect would think about and design a new building. A building is constructed of a series of interlocking and interdependent parts such as the foundations, lifts, air conditioning system, foyer, gardens and so on, and an organization has to be similarly conceived. Some managers cannot understand how the various parts of the organization are connected in order to function in the best way. Others can appreciate this concept, which can be a cause of disunity.

Functionalism. Some managers at director and executive levels in organizations are trapped in their functional specialisms. They may have spent much of their working lives as accountants, architects, surveyors or engineers and find it difficult to appreciate issues that do not support their function. Often their very success in the organization has been attributed to how well they ran, built up and looked after the interests of their function. They evaluate all decisions or possible courses of action against the effect that they will have on that particular function. Their protectiveness towards their function is sometimes to the detriment of the organization as a whole and does not foster management unity.

Lack of clear management philosophy. Some managers are pragmatic, oriented towards day-to-day results and have little interest in or fascination for understanding and developing clear management philosophies. In the same way that some people are passionate about great art, others are enthusiastic about racing cars. Similarly with management philosophy, some managers have a very clear view of how the organization should be run, while others have no view, or there may be managers with opposing ideas. In both cases the progress of the change programme can be hindered as a result of the different opinions.

Piecemeal projects. Frequently managers will embark on a change project without fully considering their objectives and the steps that are necessary to bring about the changes that they desire. A typical example of this is a teamwork project, when a manager may think that running a workshop will make the employees a cohesive and fully functioning team. Nothing could be further from the truth. Teamwork can take a long time to develop and not one but several interventions are necessary to build the team. In addition, real teamwork has to be supported by a certain culture and management style to be effective. If projects are introduced without being fully considered then they will only be of limited success and management disunity can result.

Inadequate preparation. Undertaking significant change is a complex task and should not be started without careful and thorough planning. Good preparation has a number of elements. Many organizations begin the process by systematically visiting consultants, other businesses and experts who have followed a similar route. Managers find out what changes have taken place, how they were implemented and the results achieved. Based on this information they are able to assess what is feasible for their own situation and developing philosophy. A second aspect of good preparation is for the management team to reach a full understanding of what they are attempting to achieve and how they envisage the shape and style of their organization in future years. This is a lengthy process and can take many hours of discussion and debate. The timescale for the change must also be realistic. It can take several years to change the culture of an organisation so that people think and behave in different ways. Again, thinking, planning and preparation has to go into the different phases of change over the years so that the optimum benefits are achieved.

Self-centred managers. Some managers find it difficult to think and behave collectively rather than individually. They are more concerned to satisfy their own needs and desires than those of the team. If they have grown up in a competitive environment, then their success has often depended on winning at the expense of others. Their kind of behaviour may benefit them but it can cause great disruption to the management team. Issues such as these have to be confronted and worked through and eventually an ethos has to develop in which the team is greater than any one individual. This is important not only for the health of the team but also for the image that is presented to the rest of the organization. There is little point in attempting to develop a new team-based culture in an organization if its designers and implementers cannot act as a unified team.

Your organization

Having considered the importance of management unity and some of the reasons for disunity, now assess your change programme in a number of areas. First complete the Unified Management Vision Questionnaire on pages 65–67. Read the instructions and if necessary refer to the notes that you made on the Change Process Profile on pages 16–19.

When you have completed the questionnaire examine your scores on each element. Pay particular attention to the high and low scores. Try to assess the reasons for the high scores. What are the relevant circumstances and how can they be transferred to other situations for the benefit of the organization?

When examining the low scores identify the factors which are acting as negative influences. Is there any way they can be reduced? If necessary make notes in the space provided.

The next stage of this examination of unified management vision is for you to examine yourself – the role you play, the attitudes you show and the behaviour you display. Complete the short questionnaire, Am I Playing My Part? which starts on page 68. Please follow the instructions given.

In completing the two questionnaires, Unified Management Vision and Am I Playing My Part, you have examined both the broader organization issues and your individual contribution. Turn your thoughts into actions by filling in the action plan on page 70.

Summary

Factor four, Unified Management Vision, examined the importance of unity and some of the problems which impede it. You have assessed your current level of unity and also your personal contribution. Based on your comments and scores on the questionnaires you have written an action plan for improvement.

Refer to the Change Process Profile on page 15 and if necessary adjust your percentage confidence score in relation to the new understanding you have reached after completing this section.

Unified management vision questionnaire

Completing the questionnaire

This questionnaire will help you to assess the unity and effectiveness of the change champion and the change team. Read the statements at each end of the scale then mark with a cross ☒ where you think you are for each area. Your score will be between 1 and 7. If necessary make notes to support your score in the space provided.

---

1. Defined team

There is no champion or team responsible for implementing the change programme.

1	2	3	4	5	6	7

There is a champion who has a clearly defined and known team responsible for the change programme.

Notes:

---

2. Unified team

The team is disjointed and fragmented with members pursuing their individual aims.

1	2	3	4	5	6	7

The team is unified, strong and cohesive with all members concentrating on organization issues.

Notes:

Reproduced from *A Manual for Change*
by Terry Wilson, Gower, Aldershot, 1994.

3. Clear vision

No clear vision has been developed of the future organization which guides the change programme.

1	2	3	4	5	6	7

The change programme is driven by a precise and clear vision of the future state of the organization.

Notes:

4. Communication

Communication of the vision is poor and people do not know where we are heading.

1	2	3	4	5	6	7

The vision is communicated effectively throughout the organization.

Notes:

5. Vision updating

Little updating of the vision takes place and people are unaware of what is happening.

1	2	3	4	5	6	7

The vision and plans are regularly updated and all people in the organization are kept informed.

Notes:

Reproduced from *A Manual for Change*
by Terry Wilson, Gower, Aldershot, 1994.

6. Commitment

Because the management change team does not function well, commitment to the change process is very low.

1	2	3	4	5	6	7

The unity and vision of the management change team have created a positive commitment throughout the organization.

Notes:

7. Ambassadors

The change team's performance and image are so poor that people in the organization are turning against the change programme.

1	2	3	4	5	6	7

The vision and enthusiasm generated by the management team are so appealing that new ambassadors of the change are being created throughout the organization.

Notes:

Reproduced from *A Manual for Change* by Terry Wilson, Gower, Aldershot, 1994.

Am I playing my part?

The ability to create a team with a unified management vision is ultimately the responsibility of every member of that team. Individuals have to ask themselves if they are contributing and doing enough.

By answering the questions below you will be able to assess how your own attitude, ability and effort are aiding or hindering the change team. Put a cross ☒ in the appropriate box.

	Yes	Sometimes	No
I can usually take the broad view of all situations.	❑	❑	❑
I like working with new ideas and concepts.	❑	❑	❑
My natural energy and enthusiasm motivate people.	❑	❑	❑
Working with others in a team gives me the greatest pleasure.	❑	❑	❑
I get bored with routine and conventional thinking.	❑	❑	❑
It is my genuine belief that we can organize how we do business in a much better way.	❑	❑	❑
Anything which releases the natural talents of people has to be encouraged.	❑	❑	❑
Good teamwork is one of the most effective ways of running an organization.	❑	❑	❑
I try to get people to see things in terms of possibilities and opportunities rather than problems and difficulties.	❑	❑	❑
When working in a team you have to take time to understand the other person's point of view.	❑	❑	❑
It is important for a management change team to show unity to the outside world.	❑	❑	❑
I relish working in uncertain situations.	❑	❑	❑
I am happy with the new approaches and philosophy which are being developed to run the organization in the future.	❑	❑	❑

Reproduced from *A Manual for Change*
by Terry Wilson, Gower, Aldershot, 1994.

Scoring the questionnaire

Allocate scores to your answers to the questionnaire as follows: Yes = 2, Sometimes = 1, No = 0. Now calculate your total score and compare it to the totals below.

Score

26 – 24   Your contribution to the team in the change process is excellent. You are an example to all.

23 – 18   You are broadly in agreement with and supportive of the team. You are a good team member.

17 – 12   Your contribution to the team and its aims could be better. You should review and discuss your concerns.

11 – 0   You have serious concerns about the team and its direction. You should discuss these with your colleagues immediately.

What does the score reveal about you? Are you satisfied or do you need to improve? Are you aiding the change process or holding it back? How are you regarded by your colleagues?

Reproduced from *A Manual for Change*
by Terry Wilson, Gower, Aldershot, 1994.

Action plan

Completing the action plan

Now that you have completed the questionnaires in this section, answer the questions below to give you an action plan for improvement.

Is the value of a unified management vision understood and recognized by the management team? What actions need to be taken?
Is the management team performing its role effectively in projecting a unified management vision to the organization? Does anything need to be done to improve it?
Am I personally supporting and encouraging a unified management vision? What actions should I take to be an even more effective team member?

Factor five: Change of organization philosophy

The key to understanding an organization is identifying the fundamental principles on which it is founded

The end of the 20th century will be remembered as a time of dramatic change when the very foundations of long-standing institutions and practices were shaken. The values and principles on which social conventions were based were questioned and sometimes overturned. The effects of this re-examination extended to the demise of the communist philosophy, the standing of the British monarchy, the ordination of women priests, property and share ownership for the British working class, a reassessment of educational values and many others.

A similar reassessment took place of how organizations should be viewed and managed. The conclusion was quite frequently reached that many of the values, principles and practices that had served over the past decades were no longer relevant. Changes had to take place which were often a complete reversal of what had previously been accepted. Such changes could not be effectively brought about by a modification to a system or a new management directive; they were fundamental to how people thought about organizations, work and jobs.

Some of the reasons underlying changes in business and organizational philosophy were discussed and analysed in Factor three, The nature of change. As well as understanding the factors and forces influencing and shaping organizations, every manager must determine which changes in organizational philosophy, style and practice must be adopted to survive and be effective in today's environment. No one model of organization design exists that is applicable to all organizations and which everyone must adopt. Quite the reverse – organizations are shaped by their history, environment, markets, trading patterns and a host of other influences. However, there are a number of principles that are currently shaping management thinking and organization designs which the prudent manager

71

should seriously evaluate and consider. Some of these are described below.

Organizational vulnerability

No organization is safe from change and many are facing attack in an increasingly turbulent environment. Even prestigious organizations or whole industries can suffer dramatic decline and contract to a fraction of their former size. All that is needed is a shift in the world's political balance, a change in government policy, technological innovation by competitors, the disappearance of a main market or an alteration in consumer taste. Organizations therefore have to be designed to be highly responsive to their environments. They should have sensitive antennae which detect changes and a management style which enables them to change direction or shape.

Manageable units

Plants, factories or units have to be of such a size that they are not too complex to manage. Massive units employing many thousands of people were normal in the pre- and post-Second World War periods. They were originally built to capitalize on economies of scale and were run on scientific management principles. However, the decision makers were too remote from the shop floor, the structures were too complicated and confusing, and the lines of communication were so long that they caused distortion. One of the greatest failings of this kind of organization was that work was meaningless for many employees. Individual work tasks had been dissected to such an extent that it was almost impossible to understand their role in the making of the product. To counteract these kinds of difficulties, organizations since the 1980s have developed much smaller, integrated business units, often based on clear and identifiable products. As far as possible each unit is responsible for its own output, profitability, resources management and organization. This leads to a greater sense of identification and integration for all those who work in the units.

Encouraging and rewarding differences or similarities

Many organization designs and management philosophies have unintentionally encouraged the expression of differences rather than similarities between people. This extends to, for example, different styles of dress, different terms and conditions of employment, different eating arrangements, different pay structures, different working hours and so on. It is almost as though an unconscious policy has been adopted to eradicate similarities, which is clearly not a philosophy that should be encouraged for the organization of the future. Firstly, it is out of step with the move towards equality taking place in society as a whole. There is no doubt that there has been a questioning of many values to do with class, status and equality which has influenced how people see their relationship with others in the organization.

A second and perhaps more pragmatic point is that it is intellectually unsound to expect people to pursue the same aims in an organizational philosophy based on differences. Therefore many organizations are adopting policies of harmonization in which mechanisms and procedures for emphasizing differences are being abandoned. There are now many single-status restaurants and canteens, non-reserved car parks, open-plan offices, standard work attire, equalization of holidays and working conditions. Organizations which pursue this philosophy of similarities are benefiting from greater harmony, increased output and improved quality.

Flattening of hierarchies

Traditional organizations are made up of many levels of employees, like the layers of a cake, one on top of the other. Each layer has its own status and conditions of employment, which uphold the philosophy of differences. Current thinking leads to the removal of as many levels as possible in an attempt to rid the organization of bureaucracy. This provides faster and more accurate communication channels both up and down the organization with less chance of distortion.

Another benefit of flattening hierarchies is that individual units can be more autonomous and responsive to their customers' needs. Within the general policy guidelines of the organization, managers are able to take decisions that previously would have had to be referred to more senior managers.

Perhaps one of the greatest benefits of removing layers is that unit managers and employees feel a far greater degree of identification with their particular operation. They have an entity for which they are partly responsible and they succeed or fail through their own efforts. The buck stops with them.

Empowering individuals

For many organizations empowerment has been one of the most important features of their new philosophy. It involves a realization that no matter how energetic, effective and competent the managers of a business are, on their own they cannot do all the thinking and run an effective organization. Managers today have to adopt a philosophy, set policies and create cultures that allow the abilities and talents of every person to be expressed and harnessed. People must be empowered and given support to innovate in their jobs. There should not be a marked distinction between an individual's private life and their working experience. All the talents that they use to run their lives, homes, families and outside interests are available to the organization and form a vital resource which the organization should draw on. If this is done both the organization and the individual benefit.

Empowerment can be likened to motivation, which is an important skill for any manager. Empowerment, however, is a much broader concept which entails examining and changing many of the influences and policies that govern the design and arrangement of work in the organization. Empowerment is not achieved through management decrees or directives,

73

but through reconsidering how people are treated and managed.

Teamwork culture

The team is one of the main building blocks of many organizations and much management time, effort and resources are being invested in designing and developing interlocking and cohesive team cultures. The organizational benefits are enormous. Perhaps the greatest is the search for team and organizational synergy where the whole becomes greater than the sum of the individual parts. Teams achieving synergy can far exceed the output of mere collections of people and in so doing boost the productivity of their units and organizations.

The team is also an ideal mechanism for releasing the talents and energies of people to solve problems. Team members feed on each other's ideas and are able to develop solutions to problems that would be almost impossible for individuals to solve on their own.

Another important benefit of successful teamwork is that it can free the organization by opening channels of communication, breaking down barriers between functions and departments and generally creating a situation where change and new ideas are more readily accepted.

Leadership and management style

For teamwork and empowerment to be effective, organizations and all managers must adopt a management style that encourages and reinforces individual growth and teamwork processes. Managers have to set standards, give directions and then allow people freedom to do their work in the way they consider most effective. Managerial control is kept to a minimum while skills such as coaching, facilitation, counselling and mentoring become important for every manager. Managers concentrate on assisting people and teams to achieve their tasks rather than telling them what to do.

For some managers this will be a complete reversal of how they have managed for many years. Their status gave them authority and people acted in response to this authority. Under the new philosophy, authority is devolved lower in the organization and management status and prestige are derived from the manager's process skills and how well he or she can empower people to work and achieve the aims of the business.

Importance of customers

One of the greatest changes that the average person would have noticed about organizations in the past few years is the emphasis on customer care. There has been a remarkable recognition that the customer is important and needs to be courted and looked after. This has resulted in massive investment in customer care programmes and training. Many of these have been highly successful, resulting in a transformation of the supplier/customer relationship and increased effectiveness and profitability for the organization.

The emphasis on customer care has also extended to the relationships within the organization. Every work transaction taking place in an organization is a relationship between a customer and client. If all these are analysed and made to work effectively then the organization benefits greatly.

The reason the customer relationship has been singled out is that it is a transition point where standards of quality and output can be checked and the producer has a clear responsibility to satisfy the customer.

The quality revolution

Developed in Japan, these ideas of quality based on the work of the American Dr W Edwards Deming have led many organizations to introduce quality strategies and training policies. Organizations were losing market share to some products from Japan and the Far East whose quality was far superior. It was necessary for Western companies to respond or they would be forced out of business.

Every organization must now regard the quality of their products and services as of paramount importance and introduce measures to improve and assure high quality. It is, however, questionable how far organizations will go towards full Total Quality Management, which involves a marked change to their existing philosophy.

Developing people

Senior managers will often espouse the principle that people are the organization's most valuable resource, for without them there would be no business. While this holds true it is a paradox, because organizations have been shedding large numbers of employees since the 1980s. This has been a response both to economic conditions and to the rapid increase in automation and computerization which has occurred. Almost without exception each new computerized system requires fewer people to operate it.

Employment patterns are changing and organizations need fewer but more highly skilled people. It is with these core employees that the development effort must take place. Such people are at every level in the organization and special development programmes are necessary to ensure that they know about the business, its operating environment and the systems and procedures required to run it successfully. There should also be programmes directed at people's longer-term growth, to ensure that they do not reach a 'plateau', start to decline and become ineffective. The ethos adopted by organizations should be 'growing and developing people in a growing and developing organization'.

Your organization

Having read and thought about some of the influences that are shaping organizations' philosophies and designs, now consider your own organization. This you can do by completing the Organization Review which starts on page 77.

If necessary refer to the notes that you made on the Change Process Profile on pages 16–19.

After you have completed the review, consider your future organization by completing the Change of Organization Philosophy Action Plan on pages 80–84.

Summary

Factor five, Change of organization philosophy, discussed a number of issues and features that are shaping the future design of organizations. You have thought about these issues and then considered your own organization. You then conducted a review to identify the often invisible principles and values which form the basis for the organization's design and management behaviour. The final stage was to consider the discrepancy between present and future values and principles and the action that is necessary.

Refer to the Change Process Profile on page 15. Reflect on the exercises you have just completed and if necessary adjust your percentage confidence score on the profile.

Organization review

Completing the review

Having considered what a change in organization philosophy means and reviewed some of the principles of new philosophies, think about your own organization. To find the answer to some of the questions you may have to reflect long and hard, as you need to get underneath the day-to-day issues and identify the principles on which the organization is based. Complete all four sections of the review.

Write a slogan that expresses your current organization philosophy. Typical slogans are 'Pile it high, sell it cheap', 'Value for money', 'Innovation at all costs', 'The firstest with the mostest'.

Write below the ten values or principles on which your organization is based.

1.

2.

3.

4.

5.

6.

7.

8.

9.

10.

Write a slogan that expresses the organization philosophy you must have for the future.

Write below the ten values or principles on which your organization must be based for survival and growth in the future.

1.

2.

3.

4.

5.

6.

7.

8.

9.

10.

By completing this review you have been able to detach yourself from day-to-day issues and consider the values and principles which have shaped your organization and management thinking. In many organizations there is a discontinuity between current values and principles and those required for future growth and stability. It is the gap between the present and the future that should be the foundation of management policy. The other complication which you will have discovered as you completed the review is that values and principles can be hidden and have an invisible influence on management thinking and action. It may require considerable effort to bring the values and principles to light.

Reproduced from *A Manual for Change*
by Terry Wilson, Gower, Aldershot, 1994.

Change of organization philosophy action plan

Take each value or principle on which your organization should be based in the future and write down any actions that you feel should be taken. If there is a close alignment between present and future then few actions may be required. However, if there is a wide gap between the two sets of values and principles then this could involve your organization in considerable change over the coming years.

Value/Principle 1:

Actions:

Value/Principle 2:

Actions:

Value/Principle 3:

Actions:

Value/Principle 4:

Actions:

Value/Principle 5:

Actions:

Value/Principle 6:

Actions:

Value/Principle 7:

Actions:

Value/Principle 8:

Actions:

Value/Principle 9:

Actions:

Value/Principle 10:

Actions:

Now that this review is complete you have valuable information about the present and future state of your organization. As a manager you should think of the most effective way of feeding it into the management policy making process so that it is influential in deciding the future design of the organization.

Factor six: Change phases

Change programmes are a series of management initiated waves. The secret is to fully understand them and remain in control.

Any substantial organization development programme has a number of phases which the change champions have to initiate and implement. These phases are driven by the vision of the future state of the organization. They are:

- developing the vision;

- understanding the vision;

- accepting the vision;

- behaving according to the vision.

Each of these phases has to be carefully considered and put into operation if the change programme is to be effective. The phases are discussed below.

Developing the vision

Assuming that the change champions have assessed and analysed the current state of the organization and reached the decision that large-scale change is required, the first step is to articulate and describe its future state. The process through which the vision is developed can make a valuable contribution to the change programme. Some of the areas which have to be considered are described below.

The operating environment

For most organizations the operating environment is the first area to be considered. Organizations will only survive and be effective if they understand their market-place and satisfy their customers. This requires relevant market intelligence and constant monitoring of trends and competitor activity. How an organization reacts to and handles its market has a considerable influence on the kind of arrangements that it makes to ensure effective operations. For example, a company manufacturing and selling replacement windows will adopt a different style and culture to a local government department responsible for providing a library service. Similarly, a retail chain with several hundred small outlets will have a different market and hence organization philosophy to a business with only one unit producing millions of cans of baked beans. However, all these enterprises will design their organizations to enable them to deal with their operating environments.

Commercial objectives

Any vision will be worthless unless the organization is able to meet its commercial objectives and remain viable. There is little point in developing a vision and implementing grandiose schemes for managing the organization if it has insufficient finance to serve its customers. Therefore all the normal ratios, measures and parameters that are relevant to the organization will have to be part of the vision. This will be the case whether the organization is a motor manufacturer, a hospital, a school, an insurance company, a charity or in any other field of business.

No organization has unlimited resources, so the vision will be shaped by commercial obligations. Projects will have to be designed to suit the resources available, as will the timescale for the change programme. Time costs money and the investors will know when they expect a return on their capital. How long can they wait – two years, five years, ten years or longer?

Change champions' beliefs

While an assessment of the organization's operating environment may indicate what has to be achieved, the way the organization is designed and run is a direct reflection of the beliefs that the change champion(s) hold. Managers who are change champions are in that position because they have firm beliefs. They design their organization in the same way as they would design their house or garden, including what they feel would serve them best and what they prefer. Their beliefs and preferences can come from a variety of sources, ranging from an almost religious fervour about organizations and management to an informed view of current organizational trends.

The ideas of management theorists are perhaps one of the greatest influences on managers' beliefs and thinking. There is no shortage of 'gurus' who put forward persuasive philosophies which the change champion can adopt and use as a basis for designing the organization.

Employee empowerment

One of the greatest challenges to any organization designer is to tap all the energy and talents of every member and employee. How the change champion sees this challenge will affect the way the organization is designed and managed. Some champions believe that giving freedom and autonomy are key to motivation, while others concentrate on objectives, targets and individual financial incentives. Others can hold the view that motivation comes from working in close harmony with others in an integrated teamwork culture.

During the development of the vision there must be agreement among managers about which view they hold, as this can affect how they organize and run their departments.

Management style

The management style that is advocated in an organization is directly related to motivation and empowerment, since management style has a significant effect on employee behaviour. An attempt should be made to articulate and if possible define and measure the management style as part of the vision development process. Management style can sometimes be overlooked, yet it controls and conditions much of the interaction between people in the organization. Another reason for defining the style is that substantial change often requires managers to act in a different way. Without a definition of the style needed and a new model they have no reference points and consequently become confused about how they should manage people.

Focus

As an integral part of vision development there should be a clear understanding of what the organization is to be known for and excellent at which elevates it above its competitors. This may be a statement in a mission statement or company charter, such as:

● Secure for the company a significant and permanent advantage that will enable us to fulfil our responsibilities to the shareholders.

● Expect each person to do the right job first time.

● Build and maintain a strong sense of commitment and partnership among our employees.

● Aim to be the market leader.

● Give customers competitive defect-free products on time.

While such statements can be seen merely as words which sound good, if they are taken seriously they are important in guiding management thinking and action.

Organization and management structures

Factor five, Change of organization philosophy, referred to the trends and choices available in terms of organization design. A very important part of the vision is the decision about structure. The change champion and management team will have to consider such elements as:

Size and composition of units.

What units are based on and the degree of autonomy they have in controlling their operation.

Interrelationships between the different units.

This includes the position of service departments and support services. The unit's relationship with head office and the executive management team is also important. A further consideration is the control of resources and budgets.

Organizational levels.

The number of levels helps to determine the character of the organization, for example amount of bureaucracy, speed of communication, degree of autonomy, levels of authority and individual job structure. These also influence the degree of motivation and empowerment of both managers and other employees.

Controls and procedures

An important aspect of the vision and new organization design is an understanding of the type and style of controls and procedures that the organization requires. The first question to be addressed is the degree of control that managers have in delegating work. Many of the current management philosophies call for a loosening of management control in favour of delegation to lower level employees.

One of the reasons for procedures in organizations is to support the existing values and principles and make them work in practice. For example, clocking-on procedures express a certain perception of employees. This is even more pronounced if employees have to clock on whereas managers do not. Similarly, a payment system based on individual output and achievement encourages individual motivation which may be detrimental to teamwork.

Any vision must therefore carefully consider the existing controls and procedures in the organization to see if they are supporting or impeding the proposed new culture.

The process for developing the culture

The vision is developed through a combination of internal and external influences on the change team. The internal influences are the collective experiences of the management team and any information they have gained from books and articles, watching films and so on. Another source of internal influence is consultants who have additional knowledge and experience gained in other industries and organizations.

External influences can be the result of the management team visiting other organizations known for their forward-looking organization philosophies. Many business visions have come from such visits, not least because the vision has been seen in operation and would therefore not be a leap into the unknown.

The vision develops over time as the managers and the organization learn. Ideas are discussed and tested; those that appear feasible are developed further while others are abandoned.

As the change process continues and other managers and groups become involved, they start developing visions for their part of the organization. The original change champions should be kept informed of these visions as some may not be in agreement with the overall vision. Any variations must be identified and discussed.

One of the early strategic decisions that the change champions will have to make is how much of the new vision should be developed by the different levels in the organization. Should the approach be 'top down', 'bottom up', or a combination?. Furthermore, what should be the role of the various interest groups, particularly trade unions, in the development of the vision?

Understanding the vision

After the vision of the future organization has been developed by the change champions their task is then to help everybody in the organization to understand it. This is not as easy as it would first appear. Whereas the change champions may be enthusiastic, motivated and perhaps thrilled at the prospect of running the enterprise in a way which will ensure its future success and give everyone involved a more worthwhile and satisfying existence, others may have a different opinion. The change champions can be likened to the proud parents of a newborn baby who are euphoric and think that theirs is the best baby in the world, whereas others not so involved see it as just another baby. There will, however, be some people who will immediately understand the vision and find it immensely appealing. They will become missionaries of the change.

Some of the reasons for a lack of understanding are described below.

Lack of previous experience

There are people who can only understand something if they have experienced it in the past. Therefore as people in the organization have no experience of the new vision that is being put forward, they have no understanding of it. To them a vision which promises greater responsibility, more flexibility, setting their own targets and so on is like discussing the great virtues of an orange when they have never seen, felt or tasted an orange. They may accept the vision on faith but they cannot understand it until they have experienced its effects.

Ways of overcoming this difficulty include sending such people on visits to other organizations, showing them films of similar visions in operation and running specially designed training programmes.

Lack of involvement

One of the dangers of a 'top down' strategy, for which all the thinking and vision development has been carried out by a senior management team, is that it may be rejected or misunderstood when it is communicated to the whole organization. To prevent this happening, consideration should be given to involving various levels in the organization in the vision development process. They in turn will become change champions and help the change to be achieved.

Unappealing vision

A considerable difficulty that change makers face when instituting far-reaching change is that the result is often that the organization has to produce more, to higher standards, with less people. The people affected do not see this as a better, more rewarding or satisfying future. Their view is that they will have to work harder, suffer greater stress and take on further responsibilities. No matter how much the change champions talk about 'working smarter not harder' and making savings through technology and computerization, the credibility gap remains. In addition people have the anxiety that they may be one of those asked to leave or take redundancy.

To overcome the problems of an unappealing vision, very careful consideration has to be given to the way the vision is presented and to the compensation that will be given to those displaced by the change.

Little faith in the change champions

When significant change is necessary for survival and the change programme is being carried out by the existing managers, the statement is often heard that, 'These are the people that got us into this mess, they are certainly not the ones to get us out.' A lack of trust could also be coupled with this attitude. Such views are obstacles to change, in particular if a participative change strategy is envisaged. In this situation the change champions must either resign and bring in others who may have greater credibility, or work hard to prove the sceptics wrong.

Newness is a threat

For some people anything that disturbs the existing order is a threat and has to be rejected. No attempt is made to understand the vision. Such people block out the very possibility of change. Therefore they are the last to accept and understand the vision, often only when everyone else around them has been converted.

Visionaries are scarce

Perhaps the greatest obstacle to be overcome is that there are only a limited number of people in an organization who have natural vision. This is the ability to detach oneself from day-to-day reality and project one's mind to the future and how it could be. People who lack vision find it difficult to conceptualize the organization and its future. All visions are based on a great deal of faith and perhaps this is what the non-visionary has difficulty accepting.

The importance of understanding

For any change programme the stage of vision understanding is important.

A few people will understand immediately whereas others will take time. Some will never understand and will prefer to seek alternative employment rather than be involved in something that they do not feel a part of.

It is also the stage of the process where the change champions have to make a considerable investment of time, energy and resources in communication exercises, meetings, discussions and training events. If these are done correctly people will be clear about why they are having to change, what the future organization will be like and will have an idea of the working environment and the job they will have to perform. Achieving understanding will also make the next stage far easier to implement.

Accepting the vision

After they have reached an understanding of the vision, every person in the organization should examine their values and conscience to see if they can accept that the vision of the future being put forward is best for them and the organization. The more radical the change the more they will have to adapt their way of thinking.

In the past few decades organizations have moved from enterprises based on hierarchical status and authority to participative, egalitarian and teamwork cultures, and this has swept away longstanding practices and privileges that many people have known all their working lives. For example, managers in some organizations have been affected by a philosophy of equalization. Single-status restaurants and canteens have replaced segregated eating arrangements. In some establishments there were separate restaurants for shop floor staff, supervisors, junior managers and office staff, managers, senior managers and directors. Individual offices guarded by a secretary have been replaced by open-plan arrangements with shared clerical assistance. Even directors do not have their own office, just a space and a desk the same as everyone else.

Another example of this process is in styles of dress, where everyone including senior managers has a company uniform with his or her name on it. A stranger visiting such a place would find it difficult to distinguish the managing director from a clerical assistant.

Along with such changes different managerial and working patterns have been introduced which people have had to accept. For example, many junior managers have seen their traditional authority eroded as work teams have become responsible for many of the tasks that they previously performed. In some organizations the change has been even more radical, with entire layers of managers removed and their work either discontinued, passed upwards or delegated downwards.

The emphasis on quality and the customer has already been mentioned and this has drastically changed employees' perceptions, roles and behaviour. The purpose of quality control has had to be reconsidered in many organizations so that the producer is also responsible for quality. Customers are being treated in a different way, resulting in marked attitude and behaviour changes in some managers and staff.

Changes such as these, which could be part of an organization's future vision, have to be accepted by the people involved. If they are not accepted, then the chances of them being put into operation are slim.

Planning the process for gaining acceptance of the vision by people in the organization is a vital part of the change makers' strategy. This could involve a whole range of communication and involvement techniques including conferences, presentations, discussions, meetings, policy development forums, project teams, shop floor meetings and so on.

Some of the main reasons for non-acceptance are discussed below.

'The organization is invincible'

There are some people who believe that their organization will survive forever doing precisely what it is doing now. They point to the fact that it has been operating for many decades and will therefore be successful in the years to come. Their view is that there is no need for radical change, just a few adjustments will suffice. The vision and change programme have been concocted by the change champions for egotistical rather than genuine business reasons.

Remoteness

People at the lower levels of the organization who operate the computers, sell to customers or run the machines may be remote from and have little understanding of business strategy or organization development. They are mainly concerned with their jobs and the people around them. Therefore when the vision of the future is presented to them, much of it is remote from the world in which they have to operate. Unless it can be demonstrated how it will affect them, there is a chance that the vision will not be accepted.

'It will never happen to me'

Some people who have been with the same organization and in the same job for many years cannot imagine that they could lose their jobs even if the organization changes. They simply will not accept that they could be made redundant even though they read about organization failures and job losses every day. It is part of some people's psychological make-up that they will not accept change unless it is forced on them.

Opposing values

Large-scale change programmes often involve reviewing and changing the values of the organization. One area where this can apply is in the treatment and terms and conditions of employees. There can be a complete reversal of existing values and the practices and behaviour that have previously been common.

Imagine forcing a person to vote socialist when all their lives they have voted Conservative: they find it almost impossible to comply. Other business examples are team based rates for jobs, according to which every member of the team is paid the same, irrespective of the job that he or she does; or a manager asked to sit in an open-plan office when he or she has always had an office and a secretary. Persuading such people to accept the new vision can be difficult.

92

Opposed to change

There are people who are opposed to change of any kind. Anything that upsets their existing way of thinking or acting is resisted. They find security in the status quo and fear in the unknown and untested. No matter how well the new vision is communicated and made to look attractive, they will still resist.

Behaving according to the vision

Of the four stages in the change process the last one, behaving according to the vision, is probably the most difficult to achieve. It is nevertheless important that everyone in the organization starts to act differently and behave according to the new philosophy, otherwise the desired benefits wili not result. Some of the main aspects of behaviour change are discussed below.

Change at every level

If a new organization philosophy and methods of operating are to be effective, then every person must behave differently. The most senior managers must be missionaries and purveyors of the new thinking. Everything they do and say will pass messages to the rest of the organization. There is little point in trying to develop a culture based on, say, cohesive teams producing a defect-free product when the senior management team is in constant disarray and forever making mistakes. The example they set by their actions is of the utmost importance.

At the other levels of management a similar situation exists. They also have to behave in line with the new philosophy. This will not happen on its own: managers have to be trained in understanding and applying new operating methods. Considerable investment will be required in both formal training courses and on-job coaching so that the new culture develops and the appropriate management style is introduced.

In addition to a significant behaviour change in managers, almost all categories of employee will have to learn new skills. If a concept such as the 'internal customer' is introduced, when the work-flow through the organization is seen as a series of links between customers, then each person will be required to take care over these interactions. Everyone will need to be fully aware of the standards of service required and will be expected to perform to them. Such standards can be set for every kind of service in the organization, from the time required for a maintenance fitter to respond to a breakdown to the number of times a telephone rings before it is answered.

Discrepancy between what is said and what is done

One of the main dangers of organization change programmes, particularly those involving a change in management style, is that some managers can say one thing but do another. In any conversation they appear to understand and endorse the new order, but they still behave in the same old way. There are at least two reasons for this. Firstly, they do not, deep down, believe in the new vision. Secondly, they have not yet learnt how to operate in the new style. This kind of problem is common when a teamwork culture is being introduced in an organization and a manager runs a meeting using glaringly manipulative techniques. Everyone will be aware of what is happening and the manager may or may not be excused; much depends on the stage of development that the team has reached and its ability to confront such issues.

The change makers and everyone else in the organization should be aware of this potential problem and ensure that what people say and what they do are the same.

The long-term nature of behaviour change

Large-scale organization change can be a difficult and highly frustrating exercise. This is particularly so if significant managerial and cultural change is required using evolutionary rather than revolutionary techniques. Updating plant, systems, technology and operating procedures can take several years, but changing people's behaviour takes even longer.

The problem for the change makers is that they sometimes expect change to happen overnight, because they have the wrong concept of behaviour change. They see the process as like changing an old engine in a motor car. The car goes into a garage for a week, a new engine is fitted and after a few weeks of use it is running perfectly. In fact, the analogy should rather be to the growth of a small tree. It is planted and year by year it grows, blossoms, produces more fruit and after several years is close to maturity. Too often managers expect a week's training course to be sufficient to instil the new philosophy which, like the new engine, after a period of running in should be operating perfectly. The reality is that people and organizations do not change so easily. Existing perceptions and opinions have to be re-evaluated, behaviour which in the past has brought success disregarded and new ways of thinking and operating learnt. This is difficult for young people to achieve but even less straightforward for a middle-aged manager who has spent several decades thinking and operating in a certain way.

Continuous development

Given the long-term nature of behaviour change, one of the weaknesses often found in organization development programmes is that there is no long-term strategy for the development of people. This results firstly from a lack of understanding of the development process and secondly from a piecemeal approach to people development.

In the same way as the change champions have to take the organization through the stages of vision development, understanding, acceptance and behaving, so each person has to go through these stages for the job he or she performs. There should be a strategy for this process for all employees and the correct training and support given so that they can play their full part in the developing culture.

To counter the piecemeal approach to people development, development initiatives should be cascaded down the organization in line with the objectives of the change programme to span all employee groups. Several years should be allowed for this, but unfortunately it is usual for such initiatives to be modified, knocked off course or abandoned as management priorities change or resources become scarce.

94

Your organization

There is an old management adage which states that, in the long term the only competitive advantage that any organization has is the quality of its people. For any organization change programme it is the people who will either make it work or fail. If they do not behave in accordance with the new order, then it is often because they do not understand or accept it, which must indicate a failure of the change champions' strategy and activities.

Now that you have read about the four phases of change, consider how they relate to your organization change programme. Each phase is dealt with separately as it occurs, with actions being taken on each phase at the appropriate time. The first phase to analyse is Developing the vision and this starts on page 96. Read the instructions and then answer the questions. If necessary refer to the notes that you made on the Change Process Profile on pages 16–19.

Summary

Factor six, Change phases, concentrated on the future vision required for a changing organization and identified four phases of vision development, understanding, acceptance and behaviour. You have examined these and identified obstacles to them being introduced effectively into your organization. For each phase you have planned actions to be taken.

Refer to the Change Process Profile on page 15. Adjust your percentage confidence score if necessary based on the new insights you have acquired by working through this section.

Phase analysis: Developing the vision

Completing the analysis

This is the first change phase. Reflect on what you have read about vision development, and then consider your own organization to answer the questions in the analysis.

1. Describe the environment in which your organization has to operate.

2. Describe the characteristics of the organization that are effective for operating in such an environment.

3. What influence will resources and commercial constraints have on the change programme?

4. Identify the six main beliefs of the change champion(s) that will affect the organization design.

5.   Describe your vision for the future organization.

6.   What process will the organization adopt for developing the vision?

You now have a much clearer idea of vision development and the kind of organization that you personally envisage. The next stage is to consider how people will be helped to understand the vision. Now complete the analysis on page 99, Understanding the vision.

Phase analysis: Understanding the vision

Answer the questions below for your organization change programme.

1. Describe the actions that will be taken to ensure that everyone in the organization understands the vision.

2. What do you see as the main difficulties to be overcome by people in the organization trying to understand the vision? What special action will be taken?

Having considered how people in the organization will begin to understand the vision, complete the analysis on page 100, Accepting the vision.

99

Phase analysis: Accepting the vision

Answer the questions below for your organization change programme.

---

1. What do you see as the main obstacles to the vision being accepted?

---

2. Describe how these obstacles should be overcome.

After the vision is accepted, the next stage is for people to behave according to the vision. This phase is one of the most difficult to achieve and Factor ten concentrates exclusively on it. After reading Factor ten, Changing behaviour, you will have a far greater understanding of what influences behaviour in a change programme. At this stage, however, complete the analysis on page 101, Behaving according to the vision, based on your present understanding.

Phase analysis: Behaving according to the vision

On the chart below, identify the categories of employee who will have most difficulty in behaving according to the vision. Explain why this will be so.

Employee category	Explanation of difficulty

When you have identified categories of employee and the difficulties that you expect, think how the difficulties could be overcome by completing a general development strategy. Enter this on page 102.

101

Summarize the development strategy that should be adopted to change behaviour.

Development strategy

You have now completed one of the most important aspects of any major organisation change programme, developing and handling the vision of the future. Obviously there will be much to think about and the details have to be planned, but by completing the analysis you have made a significant start.

Reproduced from *A Manual for Change*
by Terry Wilson, Gower, Aldershot, 1994.

Factor seven:
The 10/90 rule

Visions are but dreams without sustained human energy, commitment and action

Anyone who has been involved in a substantial change programme will have observed that achieving a radical change in the way an organization operates can be a difficult and lengthy process. If it takes 10 units of the change champion's energy, skill and commitment to develop the future vision, then it takes 90 units for it to be implemented.

Several of the reasons for this have been discussed and examined in Factor six. Developing, understanding, accepting and behaving according to the vision are to some extent intellectual processes that people have to work through by themselves. The change champions also have to generate emotional commitment. Factor ten discusses in detail what has to be taken into account if the organization and individuals' behaviour is to change.

All change champions want to compress the implementation stage as much as possible and if the rule could be amended to 20/80 then it would result in significant savings in management time, effort and resources. The real key to implementation is to engage the organization in an exciting and emotional exercise that is sustained throughout the programme. Every manager knows the power of feelings in motivating people. Often people may not fully understand what is happening, but if they feel good about it then they will have commitment.

To understand in more depth how energy and commitment are generated in an organization during a change process, one needs to analyse them in relation to the phases of change and the management initiatives and actions that are taking place during each phase.

Energy/commitment level

Figure 7.1 shows the change phases and the level of energy and commitment expected from employees if there is no serious attempt to harness their feelings and emotions.

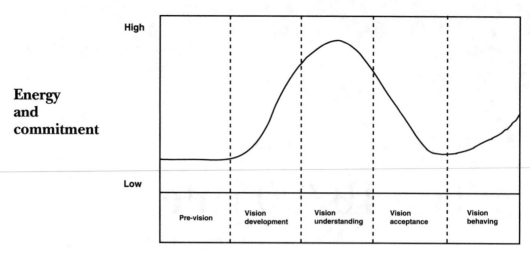

Stages of organization development

Figure 7.1   Energy and commitment profile

Every organization will have its own energy and commitment profile varying with its current position and style of development. The profile shown above is for an organization that is in need of a substantial change.

Let us examine each stage in more detail.

Pre-vision. The energy and commitment profile in Figure 7.1 is low in this stage as the organization is tired, operating in outmoded ways and not very efficient. In such an organization there is nothing to be enthusiastic about.

Vision development. The change champions now start to develop the vision, involve other managers and eventually present their vision to the rest of the organization. If this is done comprehensively and with care, enabling people to discuss, debate and respond, and if the vision is appealing, then energy and commitment levels rise considerably.

Vision understanding. As people in the organization begin to understand the vision, in particular the benefits that it will bring to them and their jobs, then energy and commitment levels can rise even more.

Vision acceptance and behaving. During the last two stages energy and commitment to the vision and the change process can begin to wane. People have to make the vision work in reality. It becomes so easy to lose faith as the grand plan starts to be implemented and problems arise. The new equipment which was to produce three times the output of the old one does not seem to work correctly. Open-plan offices which seemed so conducive to speedy communication appear to be noisy and intrusive. The teams that were built on co-operation and trust and worked so well during the training sessions somehow seem to have lost their sparkle. In consequence energy and commitment can fall considerably during these difficult and trying periods.

104

Maintaining energy and commitment

During the accepting and behaving stages of a change programme which can take several years to implement fully, it is easy for the message of the vision to be diluted or even lost as people are caught up in the day-to-day operations of the business. There is often a belief among the change champions that the vision which they see and pursue, and which they spent so much time communicating to everyone else in the organization, will continue to energize and motivate people. This does not occur unless action is taken at all levels of the organization. Suggested actions are described below.

Senior management level

The change champions must organize regular briefings and updates for the whole organization. These allow the vision to be reinforced, motivation levels kept high and fresh guidelines given for adhering to the new philosophy, organization and standards. Senior managers should also develop the practice of 'management by wandering around' so that they can talk informally with employees. This enables information to be obtained at first hand while at the same time adding to managers' credibility with the lower levels of the organization.

Middle management level

Middle managers will be actively engaged in developing the policies, systems and procedures for putting the changes into practice. To help maintain energy levels they could lead project teams on issues such as energy conservation, flexible working patterns, quality improvement, telephone techniques, internal customer relations or trade union consultation procedures. They could be involved in these activities as well as ensuring that the organization maintains its output and efficiency in order to satisfy existing customers.

With all this development activity and work taking place, it is important that middle managers do not lose sight of the vision of the organization they want. Quite often they will work exceedingly long hours and endure great stress as they attempt to do two jobs: building the new organization and maintaining the old one.

Operation/work team level

It is at the level of the work team that the greatest dissipation of commitment and energy can occur unless special attempts are made by the change champions. Communication and intellectual argument are only partially successful. What is more important is for people to see changes which benefit them taking place in their operating environment and their jobs.

The right combination of 'top down' and 'bottom up' strategy will bear fruit. If a top down policy has been adopted which has imposed changes on the work teams which are seen as making their lives more difficult, then energy and commitment levels will sink even lower. If, however, the teams themselves are able to design their working environments according to the new vision within general policy guidelines set by management, then there is a far greater chance of maintaining commitment.

Combined with this involvement there will be many other activities which have to be carried out to implement the vision. As jobs are changed and new technology is introduced, people will need to be retrained in new methods, procedures and skills. Discussion, debate and counselling should be part of every manager's repertoire, enabling them to take a real interest in their people and maintain morale.

Components of energy and commitment

Throughout the change programme, champions must remain sensitive to the levels of energy and commitment in the organization. As discussed above, when energy and commitment levels are high, change is more readily accepted and implemented. Some of the main indicators of the state of morale, energy and commitment are explained below.

Atmosphere. The atmosphere can be sensed from the first moment of entering an organization. The way people talk, react and walk gives an indication of their commitment and energy levels. When these are high there is excitement, people move quickly, communicate with gestures and genuinely appear interested in their tasks. When energy and commitment levels are low there is detachment or even depression. Little enthusiasm can be seen in people and implementing change becomes more difficult.

Empowered people. The change process should release people's latent talents and skills so that they become more independent and take decisions which improve their working practices and jobs and so that they are involved in the changes affecting them. The management style is open and trusting with help and guidance given when appropriate.

Volunteers. In organizations with high levels of energy and commitment, people volunteer themselves to take on special tasks or projects. They are willing to take risks and tackle difficult assignments knowing that they are surrounded by a supportive and helpful climate. This greatly enhances the change process because people are doing practical work on real projects.

Creativity. Generating energy and commitment also releases new ideas and creativity in the organization. People attempt to break down existing conventions and methods of doing things. Innovation and new ideas are actively sought and encouraged by managers and team leaders, and contributors receive both tangible and intangible rewards in the form of both financial and organizational recognition.

Self-management. If there is high commitment and energy there is also far greater self-management by people in the organization. They are inspired by the changes, know their roles and actively pursue goals that are in line with the changes taking place. The management role moves from one of controller to one of guider, assister and coach.

Open communication. One of the benefits of increased commitment and energy is far greater communication between different hierarchical levels and between functions in the organization. Individuals will want to talk about what they are doing, knowing that others will be interested and can learn from the experiences.

Risk taking. In an energized and committed organization, more risks are taken than in one that is in a state of depression and low morale. Risks are not only related to business decisions but also involve individuals taking personal risks with their colleagues or in managerial situations. People behave like this because innovation is encouraged and it is seen to be healthy for mistakes to be made, albeit not too many!

Care. All change programmes have to have the aim of satisfying customer requirements and maintaining the highest standards in products and services. In the committed and energized organization, people genuinely care about standards and do their utmost to keep them at the highest levels possible.

Your organization

Now that you have read about the benefits of energy and commitment and the importance of the 10/90 rule, measure the level of energy and commitment to your change programme by completing the Energy and Commitment Index on page 108.

If necessary refer to the notes that you made on the Change Process Profile on pages 16–19.

Summary

Factor seven, The 10/90 rule, explained the tasks and resources required to translate the vision into behaviour. By maintaining high levels of energy and commitment during the change process this task can be made easier. You have measured the energy and commitment in your organization and planned action to maintain or improve them.

Refer to the Change Process Profile on page 15. When you have completed the Energy and Commitment Index and the action plan adjust your percentage confidence score if appropriate.

Energy and commitment index

Completing the index

Answer the questionnaire based on your knowledge of the organization. This may be confined to one section, department or function, or it may be the entire organization. The questionnaire is a series of statements and you have to allocate up to 10 points to each statement. If you fully agree with the statement score 10 points. If you totally disagree with the statement score 0 points. If you are in partial agreement then award points accordingly.

Statement	Points allocated (0 to 10)
Atmosphere. The atmosphere in our organization is full of energy and people are committed and lively. This breaks down barriers and helps the change process.	
Empowered people. The change process has released the skills and talents of people in the organization. They are fully committed to improving themselves and making the change effective.	
Volunteers. There is so much interest in and enthusiasm for the change programme that people volunteer to run projects and be members of project teams. This allows progress to be made in the changes that we are making.	
Creativity. There are many new thoughts, ideas and techniques generated in the organization. These are of great value to the change programme.	
Self-management. As such a clear direction has been given in the change programme, people are able and allowed to manage themselves. This helps with the process of change.	
Open communication. Communication in the organization is very open. People say what they think and feel. This enables us to discuss any problems or issues affecting change.	
Risk taking. Individuals are willing to take risks in our organization knowing that they will not be punished if a mistake is made. Such decisions add interest, motivation and enterprise to our programme.	
Care. Even with the changes taking place, people care greatly about the general quality of their work and upholding standards. Such attitudes and behaviour are inspired by the change process.	

Having allocated points on the eight factors, score and interpret the index accordingly.

Reproduced from *A Manual for Change*
by Terry Wilson, Gower, Aldershot, 1994.

Interpreting the index

You have allocated up to 10 points on each of the 8 indicators of an energized and committed organization. Add the individual scores together to arrive at a total. Write the total in the box.

Energy and commitment index ☐

Your score can be interpreted as follows:

Energy and commitment index

80 – 60	High	This score shows a high level of energy and commitment to the change process. It will help with the introduction of new thinking and behaviour and reduce the amount of effort required on the implementation side of the 10/90 rule.
59 – 26	Medium	This score shows a medium level of energy and commitment. The 10/90 rule is applicable to you. You should be thinking of new ways to increase energy and commitment.
25 – 0	Low	This is a low score for energy and commitment. You will have a struggle to implement your change programme and retain the commitment of your people. The implementation side of the 10/90 rule is increased for you. A drastic review of your change strategy is required.

The next stage is to use the index to assist with your change programme. Complete the action plan following the instructions.

Reproduced from *A Manual for Change*
by Terry Wilson, Gower, Aldershot, 1994.

Action plan

Completing the action plan

Now that you have worked through this section you will have begun to understand the 10/90 rule and the importance of maintaining a high level of energy and commitment in your organization. Following your assessment you should plan for improvements by completing the following sections.

---

1. The 10/90 rule

What does the rule mean to you and your organization? Have you given it sufficient thought? Do you appreciate the effort and resources that will be necessary to translate the vision into actual behaviour? Detail actions to be taken.

Reproduced from *A Manual for Change*
by Terry Wilson, Gower, Aldershot, 1994.

2. Energy and commitment index

What does your score on the index indicate? Which are your weakest areas? What will you do to improve them?

Factor eight: Transitional management

Management style and organization change are inextricably linked

There is sometimes an assumption in change programmes that most managers will automatically be attracted to the new ideology and start behaving and managing accordingly. Typically the change champions think that some of the older managers may have fixed attitudes and could experience some difficulty, but the younger ones will be the disciples of change. This is a naive assumption which underestimates the nature of organizational leadership and the process required to change it.

The leadership norms and style of the organization are the equivalent of the sap running through a tree. The sap is not readily visible but it is essential to the life of the tree. Leadership styles will have developed over many years and young managers are progressively trained in the organization's way of getting work done. Managerial behaviour patterns will have been built up which are automatic and familiar. Even if the behaviour is now inconsistent with the new organization style, it cannot be changed overnight. Firstly, people's behaviour is often difficult to change and sometimes impossible. Secondly, people are often unsure of what they are required to change to, which is the essence of the problem. A coherent picture of the new management style has not been developed and therefore cannot be conveyed to managers. They are left in limbo, each with impressions of what they possibly should do but no concrete model to follow. Coupled with this is the potential decline in organizational efficiency while people struggle to adopt the new styles, which brings pressure from senior managers for better short-term results. The manager's reaction is to revert to the practices found to be successful in the past, which frequently involves greater direction and control of the work team, and is contrary to the new philosophy and managerial style being advocated.

Organizations implementing change programmes must therefore recognize that management style is fundamental to success and take the time to

113

develop ideas and concepts that all managers can follow. At the same time, it has to be understood that changing a style is a process that can take several years. Therefore, there has to be a carefully prepared education and training strategy which reaches all managers. Some of the areas which need to be considered are discussed below.

Control and freedom

Central to the philosophy of many change programmes is the release of power and authority from the upper levels of the business to the lower levels. Decision making is pushed down as far as possible. Layers of management and bureaucracy are cut out of organizations so that jobs are expanded and enriched. The thinking behind this shift is that the people who have day-to-day control of the work know more about it and are in a far better position to make decisions than some remote person further up the hierarchy. The process is as shown in Figure 8.1.

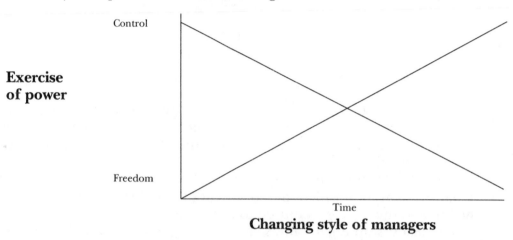

Figure 8.1   Development of managers and teams

Therefore, as control is released by senior managers at the top of the organization, freedom is gained by more junior managers and their work teams. One of the main determinants of success or failure is the ability of the managers and their teams to accept this freedom. For some people, the proposition appears very attractive: freedom from restrictions and a chance to do many other things. Others see more responsibility, increased workloads and the daunting development of a greater range of skills. This latter attitude was succinctly expressed by a forklift truck driver who was informed that not only would he be able to drive his truck, but he would also be able to select which trucks would be purchased. He dismissed this by saying that it was his job to drive the trucks and management's responsibility to buy them, a validation of the phrase 'fear of freedom'. But would he have felt the same about purchasing his own motor car? What is it about organizational life that has created this attitude?

Before the vision can be turned into reality, people have to be able to accept a larger job and more responsibility. This does not happen overnight and is a process which can take many months or even years. In the first instance, the way that people see their old job has to be gradually changed,

114

and training events help to achieve this. The manager of the work group is a key person in bringing about this change. Through a slow process of discussion, debate, argument and cajoling, people come to accept that the new approach is feasible and agree to try it.

Another significant barrier to the release of freedom in unionized organizations is the demarcation between operatives and skilled craftspeople. Both groups realize that the practices they adopt do not make sense. Machinery is stopped causing lost production while waiting for a craftsperson to make an adjustment which could easily be done by the machine operatives. Operatives are often only too willing to do what is necessary, but custom and practice decree that it is the province of skilled people.

In a similar vein, demarcation also exists between different craftspeople, fitters and electricians. However, significant inroads are being made in these areas through negotiation and multi-skilling programmes. These issues are relevant because they impede the change process and restrict the release of freedom and discretion to managers and their teams. It all takes time and adds to the frustrations of the change makers.

Another problem which adds to the resistance to change is overt hostility to management initiatives. For a variety of reasons, there are some people who take a very bloody-minded attitude to the total change process. This often occurs within the context of changes that have taken place in the past and results in statements such as 'The management are squeezing us again', 'We are being asked to do more for the same money', 'Another new broom trying to sweep clean'. Again, managers have to attempt to overcome this resistance. Obviously it is at such points that faith in the new vision is tested. It is so easy to give up and revert to old thinking and practices. Managers in this position must draw on the strength of the change team and discuss, argue and debate until they convince the sceptics and doubters.

The managers and change makers not only have to bring about significant changes in their workforce, but must also change their own role. They have to devolve decision making and authority, and release information that has seemed their reason for existing throughout much of their working lives. No wonder they often feel vulnerable without a thorough understanding of their role in the new regime. They do have a very significant and exciting role if only they can understand and adapt to it, and this is depicted in Figure 8.2 overleaf.

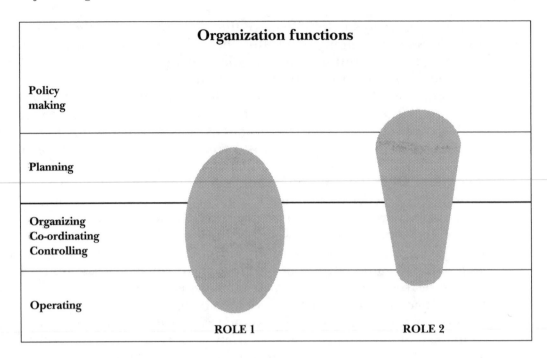

Figure 8.2   Managerial role change

Figure 8.2 uses the main functions of an organization to show the changed role of the manager. This can be explained as follows:

Policy making. Policy making is normally the province of senior managers and directors. They set the strategy and overall plans in relation to products, markets, expansions, acquisitions, capital expenditure and the general direction of the business.

Planning. Once the policy has been set then less senior managers plan its implementation. Their job is to ensure that the new product is developed and launched properly, or that the new computer system is implemented successfully and on time.

Organizing, co-ordinating, controlling. Following the successful planning of a policy initiative, more junior managers take it over and make it work on a day-to-day basis. They have to make the necessary corrections and adjustments, train and organize their staff and achieve the set targets.

Operating. Lastly there is the function of carrying out the work in contact with the customer or operating the machine. Depending on the organization's particular products and services the manager is likely to have a group of people doing the work, be they bank counter staff, salespeople or waitresses.

The manager's former role (role 1) involved planning, organizing, co-ordinating, controlling and operating functions. The new role (role 2), however, is noticeably different with a shift upwards in the manager's activities. He or she is now much more involved in planning and even has some policy-making responsibility. To enable this change to take place, some of the

116

lower-level functions of organizing, co-ordinating, controlling and operating have been delegated to other managers or to the operating teams themselves. There has therefore been a fundamental shift in the manager's role.

This shift does not occur overnight and is not as clearly defined as shown in the diagram. The reality for many organizations and managers is that they struggle and stumble towards the new role without having a clear idea of what they are aiming at. Other organizations remove a layer of management, for example first-line supervisors, and other managers and working teams have to fill the gap.

The new management role evolves slowly because of two important factors. Firstly, more senior managers must let go of the reins, change their jobs, delegate and give more authority and responsibility. To do this they must have fully accepted the new management philosophy and have great faith in their subordinates. Secondly, the manager's team must be willing and able to do part of their leader's old job so that he or she can concentrate on other, higher-level matters.

None of this can happen unless the organization's procedures and systems are also changed. Every position in a business is supported by information and systems. When there is a dramatic change in role, then this information and support must be given to new people as appropriate. This could involve informing other managers, suppliers, customers, changing computer programmes, modifying meeting procedures and generally adapting to the changed circumstances.

To summarize, gradual transformation of role is required which needs to be understood and carefully monitored if the change programme is to be successful.

Change in objective

To support the change in role, there must also be a change in the objective of every manager's job. This becomes even more necessary in the context of the trend towards Total Quality Management and quality improvement which is sweeping organizations at present. These initiatives can only be achieved if managers develop an 'improvement' perception to their thinking. All too often organizations, managers and employees accept existing methods of operating as normal, whereas the opposite should be true. They should be restless to question, overturn or improve existing methods, with continuous improvement as the goal.

It is, however, obvious that an individual manager cannot do this alone, there must be support at the highest level in the organization. Quality missions and policies have to be agreed and mechanisms to achieve them implemented, for example quality committees and improvement teams. Relevant information on quality performance also has to be communicated freely to all employees so that they are aware of their progress.

Transitional management also requires managers to maintain a clear distinction in their minds between the styles of leadership, managership and teamship. They must know how each fits into the different stages of the change programme and when they would use which, and develop the skills to use them correctly. These styles are discussed in more detail in the next section.

In the context of fundamental organization change, one important aspect of leadership is to point the way forward with confidence. For change to be successful, all managers must subscribe to and support the new vision. Changes are implemented gradually within the organization, so every manager must be an ambassador and missionary of the change. There will be many discussions and debates at all levels during which understanding has to be gained, doubts erased, and faith and belief in the change programme displayed. After all, many managers, unless they have previously been through a similar programme, have no experience of the outcome. They, like the change initiators at the top of the organization, are propelled forward by their vision.

Leadership, managership and teamship

Not only must all the managers understand and slowly develop into their new role, which determines their function, they must also decide how to operate on a day-to-day basis. How they act will vary according to the degree of understanding that their team has of the new ways of working. The manager has to operate flexibly and develop a style over time as the change process is implemented. Figure 8.3 shows that the manager can adopt one of three principal styles, which relate to the degree of certainty that each team has about their new working methods.

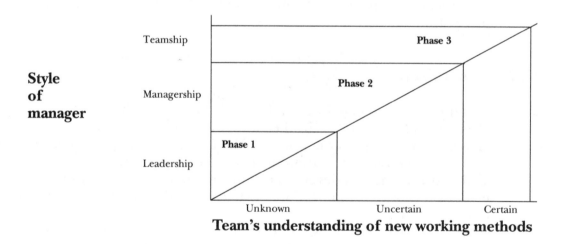

Figure 8.3   Development of managerial style

Leadership and unknown – phase 1

When the new methods of working are unknown to the team, then the manager has to adopt a predominantly but not exclusively leadership role. This involves articulating the vision of the future, painting a verbal picture of the team's work and the benefits that will accrue from greater freedom. The unknown state occurs at the beginning of the change process when there may be a great deal of fear. Team members will be apprehensive about what is going to happen. They will need discussions, explanations and reassurances. At this period of the unknown, the leader will need to display energy, confidence and a total commitment to the change. Above all, this is a time of displaying faith that what is being attempted is good for both the organization and the individual. Many people are about to have their jobs changed, sometimes out of all recognition, and faith is not something that can be touched, felt and measured. If they can only appreciate what they have personally experienced, visions of the future will have little relevance to them.

The change process is also complicated by the lengthy transition period from one method of working to the other. People are attempting to understand and accommodate the new ways while still operating in the old mode. At the same time, there is disruption all around as new plant, equipment and systems are installed, which leads to an extremely stressful working life. Furthermore, work teams can change as people are redeployed or made redundant, which adds further to the unknown.

Given these sets of circumstances, the manager has to be the leading force which holds everything together. He or she has to maintain the output and productivity of the team, keeping morale steady while slowly pushing for and introducing new working practices. At this transitional stage formal training should be designed so that it takes the team away from the day-to-day hurly-burly, where they can experience for themselves through exercises and simulations many of the features of the teamwork that the leader has been articulating. Training also gives people time to reflect and build up an image of the future.

Managership and uncertain – phase 2

As the change process progresses and changes are implemented, then the vision starts to become a reality. New plant, equipment, systems and procedures have to be operated, new skills have to be learnt and used. The transition period has begun, one of the most difficult phases for managers. They have to start producing a return on the investment in the change. The vision was easy, it was just talk; now it has to make a difference to the bottom line.

At this stage, the visionary elements of leadership are replaced by the guiding and controlling behaviours of managership. The details of the new working systems have to be understood and made to operate effectively. According to the vision, much of this is the responsibility of the work team, but the work team is inexperienced and incapable of operating alone without the old style of management support. Equipment has been installed that does not work correctly and is in need of constant attention and modification. Complex computer systems control processes and procedures that will take many months or even years to understand fully and operate effectively. To let go of the reins and tell the team to deal with the problems themselves would be disastrous.

The manager should not abandon the vision of the self-managing, self-regulating team. Many of the other elements that support and reinforce the new vision should be in place, for example, harmonization policies, team meetings and quality groups, each in their own way adding to the gradual change of culture. However, in times of uncertainty teams and individuals need structure and this can only be given by their immediate team leader.

What is important at this stage is the way that the leader intervenes and creates structure and controls. This should be done in a helpful, participative manner, rather than using an autocratic approach.

Teamship and certain – phase 3

In this phase the team has started to mature now that it understands and behaves according to the vision. Confidence has been built up as it has learnt the new systems and ways of operating. The team is able to organize itself and take decisions on running its part of the operation. The manager is therefore able to pull away from the control and direction which was invaluable during the stage of uncertainty. The main function of the manager is now to perform a role which enables the team to run itself effectively. Frequently this involves the manager becoming part of the team rather than standing above it. Now, rather than giving directions and making decisions, the manager looks after the boundaries and relationships of the team and also becomes the resource provider. The link with other teams and parts of the organization is invaluable to the team's success as it reinforces and consolidates their contribution to the wider organization.

Another valuable role for the manager is that of trainer and developer. Many motivated people need to learn and grow or they can become disinterested and less efficient. An environment must be created which is challenging and allows team members to learn new skills. This may involve attending external courses but much of the development will take place within the organization under the manager's guidance.

As the team continues to mature a good manager will become more integrated with it and act as confidant, mentor and counsellor. Trust and cohesiveness develop as members gain understanding of each other, allow for individual idiosyncrasies and achieve continual success in their outputs, tasks and targets. The transition has now taken place and the manager has attained the teamship style.

Your organization

Transitional management is an important part of any change programme. Managers frequently have to learn how to operate in a different way, particularly if the change involves a shift in organization philosophy. All managers therefore need to understand the roles that they will have to perform and acquire new skills. This requires considerable planning and investment in training. It will be examined in detail when you work through Factor eleven.

Now that you have considered the development of managerial role and style as the change process continues, apply some of the ideas and thinking to your own organization by completing the questionnaire which starts on page 122. Please follow the instructions.

If necessary refer to the notes you made on the Change Process Profile on pages 16–19.

Summary

Factor eight, Transitional management, helped you to think about the appropriate degree of management control and freedom for your organization. It also considered the managerial roles and skills required. You have made plans relating to transitional management.

Refer to the Change Process Profile on page 15. Consider the percentage score you gave transitional management when you completed the profile. Do you still agree with the score now that you have explored the subject in greater detail, or should it be higher or lower?

Transitional management questionnaire

In completing this questionnaire consider your organization and decide if you have given sufficient thought to the subject of transitional management and have planned appropriate initiatives.

1. Describe the current management style in the organization.

2. Is the current management style appropriate for the type of organization that is being developed? Please give reasons.

3. Do you envisage a change in managerial roles as a part of the change programme? If so, describe how they will change.

4. Are the concepts of leadership, managership and teamship relevant to your change programme? If so, describe how you will use them.

Having completed the questionnaire on transitional management you should now decide what actions, if any, need to be taken. Write them on the following action plan.

123

Transitional management action plan

Detail the actions that should be taken relating to transitional management.

Action to be taken	Timescale

Factor nine: Teamwork

Teamwork is the vehicle of change and sustained growth

The team is one of the main mechanisms for bringing about change in organizations. Many change initiatives are based on a teamwork philosophy in which the team becomes the central unit of the organization. The reason for using teams is that they have qualities which are ideally suited to the operating patterns of organizations. For example:

● Many tasks are too large or complex for one person to achieve alone, so a group of people must work together. The task is subdivided and each person plays a part.

● The tasks to be accomplished may involve a variety of skills and knowledge that no one person possesses. Many tasks, problems and solutions are multi-disciplinary in nature.

● Teams are capable of creating synergy, when the whole is greater than the sum of the individual parts. Synergy is the elusive quality that all managers attempt to achieve with their teams. They then have high performance that consistently exceeds set aims and targets.

● Teams create loyalty and commitment to the task and a sense of shared ownership. These qualities are generated through effective relationships within the team.

● In good teams, there is a sense of belonging and of not being alone. Problems are shared and worked out together. The mutual support greatly assists morale and cohesiveness in times of difficulty.

● Membership of different teams creates information and communication networks within the organization. The team is therefore a building block enabling people to work alone while at the same time being connected to something much larger.

● Teams are ideal for breaking down barriers between different functions and interests. When individuals are working on projects which involve numerous interest groups, tolerance and understanding are developed.

In addition, the team is the main working unit in many new organization designs. Therefore by using teams to initiate change the organization is learning the skills of teamwork, which will be invaluable for successful operations in the future.

A team defined

It is rather unfortunate that organizations can adopt a teamwork philosophy without ever really understanding how to define a team and the conditions necessary for it to operate successfully. As the old adage goes, 'If you can't define it, you can't measure it'. Many arrangements of people which purport to be teams are in fact merely groups. There is a very large difference between groups and teams. For many organizations, mature synergic teams are an ideal which is to be aimed for and only occasionally achieved. However, that is not to say that groups of people cannot be trained, helped to work far better together and produce considerable gains in output.

If you compare most teams in organizations to some of the characteristics of an ideal team you will see that they fall far short. For example, in the ideal team:

● defined targets and outputs are consistently achieved;

● leadership is shared, according to the needs of the task;

● an emotional bond holds team members together;

● there is an atmosphere of openness and trust;

● members have fun together;

● team needs come before those of individuals;

● there is a common aim, which all members share and strive for;

● all members listen to each other;

● the weaker members are helped and supported;

● there is an ethos of learning and self-development;

● decisions are arrived at by consensus;

● team roles are operated flexibly.

For a group of people to display the characteristics listed above, a number of conditions have to be present:

126

- there must be between three and eight people in the team;

- the team must meet and interact regularly;

- membership must be stable;

- member selection must be mutually agreed;

- the team must have a relevant and challenging task to achieve;

- the team must be supported by the organization;

- there must be the correct blend of technical skills;

- adequate resources must be made available to the team;

- the team must be rewarded for their efforts and success;

- the team must have a clear identity.

Therefore, for teamworking to be successful in an organization, the conditions and culture have to support team principles. A large variety of teams operate in organizations and each needs to be considered separately, since a different approach may have to be taken to its development. Some examples of different kinds of teams are discussed below.

Management teams. A management team could be a board of directors, a group of departmental managers, or managers within a department who represent their functions and meet regularly to set policy and conduct the organization's business. This is probably the most common team found in organizations and the one that people think of first when considering teams.

Workplace teams. A workplace team could comprise a group of production workers, office staff, telephone salespeople, accounts clerks or warehouse staff, with a team leader or supervisor and responsible for performing a clear and defined aspect of the organization's business.

Project teams. A project team is a group of the organization's experts selected and assembled to introduce a product, procedure, system or technique into the organization. It lasts until the project is completed and is then disbanded.

Outside/inside teams. An outside/inside team is made up of both consultants or technical experts from another organization and people from within the organization. This kind of team is used when a new idea or technique is being brought into the business from outside. Again, the team will last for the lifetime of the project.

Quality improvement teams. Quality improvement teams can take many forms, either workplace, management or cross-functional. They often have a very long life and in organizations that have adopted a Total Quality Management philosophy they produce cross-functional matrix management.

User/supplier teams. As the name suggests, a user/supplier team is a group of organization people and suppliers which meets to refine and improve the service given by suppliers and at the same time to transfer some of the organization's standards and best practices into the supplier's organization.

Employee/temporary worker teams. Organizations undergoing substantial change involving a marked reduction in the number of employees often have to bring in large numbers of temporary workers to make up for a shortfall. Some of these people can be employed for several years. Employee/temporary worker teams are led by a permanent supervisor or manager.

Changing to a teamwork culture

Any organization wanting to change to a culture based on teamwork needs firstly to have change champions who are in favour of teamwork and secondly to promote teamwork as one of its values, supported and continually reinforced by senior management. It may also be necessary to make structural changes to the groups of people in the organization so that they are able to operate as teams. It is difficult for a group of 20 people who only meet once every three weeks to operate as a cohesive work team. No matter how good the leader's intentions are, the organizational and physical conditions are inappropriate for effective teamwork.

Team leaders and members should be selected based on two main criteria. The first is the technical or commercial skills required by the team to perform its function. If the team is required to perform an accounting function, for example, then it must have the correct blend of technical skills to do the job. The second criterion is teamwork skills. There should be a blend of team skills and abilities so that members co-operate and work to make the best use of technical skills for the benefit of the team, its members and the organization as a whole.

After the teams have been defined and selected, then teamwork has to be developed by gradually training and educating everyone in the organization. This must be part of a carefully constructed strategy which should contain the following elements: the cascade principle, team training and team leader training.

The cascade principle

One design which allows teamwork to flourish is based on a series of interlocking teams from the top to the bottom of the organization. This is illustrated in Figure 9.1

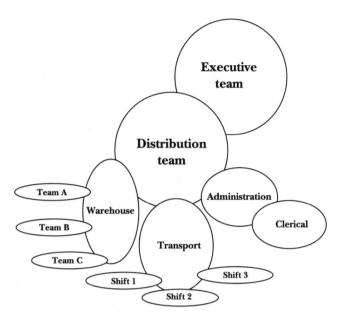

Figure 9.1   The cascade principle

In this kind of arrangement each team leader is also a member of a higher level team, for example the warehouse team leader would also be a member of the distribution team. Following the same principle the distribution team leader would be a member of the executive team. These links ensure that each team overlaps with those above and below, helping information to flow quickly from the top to the bottom of the organization and vice versa.

Following the cascade principle, first the executive team is trained in teambuilding and teamwork principles. The distribution team leader is a member of the team so he or she attends the training event. The training is then cascaded down the organization as the distribution team leader attends a training event with that team. Each team leader thus attends two training events and the process continues all the way down the organization. In this way important links and relationships are forged between teams while every person in the organization learns about teamwork and the behaviours necessary for teams to operate effectively.

Content of team training

Training of teams is often different from other forms of training. To be effective it should concentrate on three main areas.

Teamwork principles.

Teamwork, like any other aspect of human activity, operates according to principles and skills that have to be learnt by all team members. Team members need to learn how best to organize themselves for particular tasks and the roles to adopt for the most effective way of working together. In doing this they agree relationships between each other and working procedures

129

which members respect and adhere to. These principles act to lubricate the team and so ensure skilled and efficient performance.

Individual skills and insights.

Individual people are the building blocks of teams and for a team to function effectively there should be a deep understanding between team members. This understanding should incorporate not only their technical and commercial skills but also aspects of them as people and their personality. The team training should therefore be designed so that members are able to get to know each other much better than is usual in working relationships. This enables each person to share a little of themselves with the others and in so doing to begin to develop strong links and lasting relationships. The process adds an element of emotion which is the basis of cohesiveness and loyalty.

Organizations.

All teams must realize that they are part of the larger team of the total organization. When a team has undergone training and motivation, emotion and spirits are running high, they can easily forget that other teams are their customers and that co-operation with them is essential for organizational success. Therefore the team should understand how organizations are designed and function. In particular, they need to know the rationale for selecting a teamwork culture as opposed to any other form of organization design, and also the benefits that teams bring to both the organization and the individual.

Team leader training

It is often assumed that when a team leader attends team training with their team this will equip them to run the team effectively. This is not the case, as leaders have to be given particular help in their leadership role. As discussed in Factor eight, Transitional management, in the change process the leader has to go through the phases of leadership, managership and teamship and must be able to switch between modes according to the team's state of development. To do this, the leader has to assess the team's understanding of the new operating philosophy, their technical competence, their personal maturity and any individual needs that may exist.

The leader must be fully supported so that they are helped to understand their role, particularly during the transition period, and are able to cater for the needs of both the team and individual members.

Your organization

Reading this section on teamwork has given you a greater understanding of teams, how teams are used in a change programme and the help and support they need to be given. You are now in a position to assess the use of teamwork in your programme and this can be done by completing the questionnaire on page 132.

Refer to your notes on the Change Process Profile on pages 16–19.

Summary

Factor nine, Teamwork, highlighted some of the main features of teamwork and how teams can be used in your organization. Means of introducing a teamwork culture were discussed, including the training of teams and their leaders. Plans were made for developing teamwork in the organization.

Refer to the Change Process Profile on page 15. Consider your score on the profile and whether it should be changed after completing this section.

Teamwork questionnaire

Completing the questionnaire

Answer each question based on your knowledge of the organization.

---

1. Write down the main reasons for your using teams and teamwork.

---

2. How will teams help in the change programme? What types of teams will be formed?

3. What strategy will be used for forming and selecting teams?

4.   How will teams be trained?

5.   How will leaders be trained?

Factor ten: Changing behaviour

Without a change in behaviour there is no change

In essence change programmes are aimed at changing behaviour. If people do not change and achieve tasks more effectively and efficiently, then the programme will have failed. Changing the way that people behave is not, however, the easiest task. In any one organization there are many influences which have shaped behaviour and reinforce existing behaviour patterns. For a manager or a trainer to run a training course and then expect the participants to show marked behaviour changes is to misunderstand the complex nature of organizations and people. Figure 10.1 identifies the main influences that have to be taken into consideration when attempting significant organizational change.

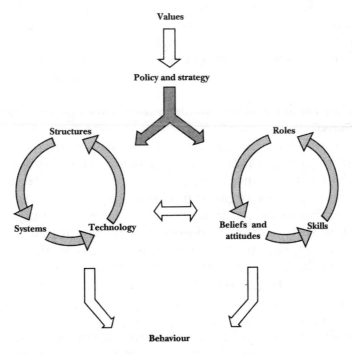

Figure 10.1 Influences on behaviour

Values

Values were discussed and analysed in Factor five. They are the foundations of any organization and they make up the organization's philosophy. Values are enshrined in mission statements and work almost invisibly, influencing the organization and each individual's behaviour. They are, however, not always of benefit. They create sense, understanding and structure for people in the organization and therefore give them a base from which to operate. In this respect they are extremely beneficial. Some values can nevertheless be detrimental to organizations which are experiencing radical changes in their markets and operating environments. The values can freeze people's perceptions, thinking and actions and prevent them from making the changes that are necessary to deal with their new circumstances.

The values which the change champions hold are extremely important as they set the pattern for the future organization. They will affect how people behave at all levels. As well as people being aware of what the change champions' values are, they must consider whether there is a discrepancy between words and actions. Sometimes champions will espouse certain values, such as product quality and excellence at all times, yet when the pressure is on and targets have to be met they send out products that do not meet their exacting standards.

Policy and strategy

Whereas organizations' and change champions' values can be invisible and have to be teased out, policy and strategy are the organization's stated intentions. Policies, strategies and plans will be developed for every area of operation, such as marketing, product development, financial management and human resource development. These will be discussed, analysed, dissected and re-appraised at the highest level.

There will be various project leaders and teams all working to implement the strategy, push the organization forward and produce the anticipated benefits. In many organizations regular briefings will be held with all staff to update them on progress and inform them of any changes to the strategy and plans.

There will therefore be two processes operating – one maintaining the outputs to the customer on a day-to-day basis, the other designing the organization for the future. These two processes will create the objective for every person in the organization and shape what they do and how they do it. These processes, particularly shaping the future organization, should be consistent with the new philosophy being developed. For example, if a culture of enterprise and innovation is a strategic aim for the organization, then both these elements should be built into the process so that managers and employees begin to understand them and practise developing them in their sections and departments. Everyone should be aware of not only what to do, but also the way to do it.

Introducing new policy and strategy initiatives can be extremely influential in shaping people's behaviour, and their importance has to be realized by everyone involved in the change process.

The organization – structures

The way an organization is structured can greatly affect manager and employee behaviour. In a traditional, hierarchical organization that has many layers of employees organized in functions with respect for authority and status, behaviour is systematized, ordered, generally risk free and follows the rules and codes that are part of bureaucratic structures. If the change champions' goal is to change the organization so that it is responsive to customer needs, creative and adaptable, then there will have to be a change of structure to allow such qualities to develop and operate.

Behaviour is conditioned by the structures in which people operate. The principal question to ask is, 'What kind of behaviour do we want to encourage?', and then the structure should be designed to encourage that behaviour.

The organization – systems

In the same way that structures either encourage or inhibit behaviour, so also do the many systems and procedures that operate in organizations. Systems and procedures are the means by which work is done. For example, there will be a system for paying people, for planning production, for controlling absenteeism, for allocating pool cars, for creating budgets and so on. Many of these systems will have been running for years and become the accepted way of operating. In any change programme, especially if there is a change of philosophy, some systems will encourage behaviour that is opposite to that required to introduce and sustain the new culture. For example, an organization may wish to develop a culture of teamwork and co-operation and attempt to do this with expensive training and team coaching, but with a payment and reward system based on individualism. In such a system people's pay is geared to individual achievement and they are encouraged to compete with others in a win or lose confrontation. To support the new culture the payment system will have to be modified to develop teamwork and therefore reward people for attaining team as well as individual goals.

Other examples of systems that are inconsistent with organization cultures seeking greater individual responsibility and involvement are those in which quality inspectors check operators' work unnecessarily, or those which incorporate different conditions for workers and staff. Many of these systems were developed to support former managerial ideologies, but unless they are modified or removed the required culture change will not take place.

The organization – technology

In this technological age, every new installation of equipment or plant, computer system or business method is more advanced and generally faster and more efficient than the one it is replacing. Many organizations are far more efficient than they were a decade ago. Far greater skill is required to design, maintain and run the new technology and it demands different

137

behaviour.

Any proposed change in an organization's philosophy or management style must be related to the effect that any new technology will have on behaviour. If jobs are to be completely de-skilled with new operating systems, then how are working interest and commitment to be maintained? If warehouses are to be fully automatic, what is the appropriate management system to support the philosophy? If production lines are automated so that operatives spend eight hours behind a console viewing a computer screen with little human contact, how is the job to be enriched and interest maintained? The relationship between technology and behaviour has to be considered in any change programme.

The individual – roles

The roles that managers and other employees adopt have a significant effect on how they carry out their work and consequently their behaviour. All too often managerial roles develop in a 'hit and miss' manner based on the amount and type of work that the manager has to accomplish, the practices learnt and found to be successful in the past, and personal values and ideologies. The role adopted and the accompanying management style become automatic for most managers, just like walking or driving a car. Once patterns of behaviour have been learnt, it requires a great deal of personal insight, analysis and determination to change them.

Particularly if the change programme involves a change of management role and style, there must be a clear definition of what managers should do and how they should do it. This needs to be backed up with extensive training and coaching. Unless this happens there will be no consistent management approach and managers will rely on outdated roles and styles which could be opposite to the philosophy advocated in the change programme.

There should also be the same clarity of thought in relation to the roles of all the other people in the organization. If it is not possible for every job in the organization to be defined, then there must be an understanding of job roles in relation to levels of responsibility, freedom, degree of trust and broader parameters consistent with the organization philosophy being developed.

Unless the roles and jobs in the organization are redesigned to fit the objectives of the change, they may act as barriers to the new behaviour required from everyone.

The individual – beliefs and attitudes

Organizational change cannot be achieved without a significant change in people's beliefs and attitudes. There will be no consistent and lasting change in behaviour unless people actually believe in what they are doing and the way they are being asked to do it. Many change programmes concentrate on aspects such as quality, customer service, teamwork or increased responsibility, which all try to alter the way employees think and act. If people are to give excellent and consistent service to a customer, they have to believe that this is in their interests and the interests of the organization. They must care about and get satisfaction out of the transaction with the customer. If in the past the customer has been regarded as a necessary evil rather than the organization's life-blood, then a significant change has to take place in this perception.

Similar changes in beliefs and attitudes may have to take place at every level in the organization. Senior managers must believe that the new approach is viable, junior managers must trust their people, team leaders must believe that the teamwork method is correct, quality managers' attitudes must change to give production people responsibility for quality standards, managers must believe that personal empowerment is the right way of motivating people, and so on.

One of the keys to persuading people to change their beliefs and attitudes is for them to gain a new appreciation of the subject under consideration. They have to change their perception and realize the benefits to be gained by behaving differently. This cannot be achieved by commanding or telling, it is a process based on discussion, debate and education, and time must be allowed for it in the change programme.

The individual – skills

Change always entails learning new skills. For senior managers these are skills associated with the changes in orientation, organization and style that they may be introducing. If, for example, they are introducing a new culture based on enterprise, innovation and excellence, they have to be models for these qualities, demonstrating in practice the new management style. Without a strong and powerful lead from the top it is unlikely that others will understand and practise the new philosophy.

It is often at the middle levels of management that the greatest changes and skill development have to take place. Radical change programmes often result in substantial restructuring of middle managers' jobs through the removal of one or more layers of management. This is frequently associated with more homogeneous structures with less emphasis on functions. All the changes have to be comprehended and managed. In addition, there may be a move to work teams which require less traditional management control and direction but more freedom and autonomy. Finally, there may be some substantial changes in the technology associated with the work processes, often computer based. All this creates many learning needs for middle level people. Without a lot of training, help and support they have difficulty in coping effectively with the new demands they face.

At the work team level, the new skill requirements can be as significant as at the middle manager levels. Many change programmes are aimed at creating a far more flexible, perceptive, quality-aware workforce and to achieve this there have to be some radical changes to the way work is done. This can mean a breakdown of traditional trade and skill categories, the introduction of computer systems which eliminate the need for many jobs, and delegation of managerial discretion and responsibility. In these circumstances the need for training in new skills can be very substantial.

Your organization

Now that you have studied the behaviour model and considered some of the influences involved, reflect on your own organization. Decide where the greatest resistance will occur to the behaviour change that is required. Complete the Behaviour Resistances exercise on page 141.

It may help to refer to the notes that you made on the Change Process Profile on pages 16–19.

This analysis is one of the most significant in this manual. A marked change in people's behaviour is something that can prove elusive.

The real test for a behaviour change initiative is whether people are motivated to change or forced to change. Forced change is frequently short lived and people quickly revert to their past behaviour. Motivated change is the result of the change champions understanding the influences and then adapting the current policies and initiatives accordingly.

Summary

Factor ten, Changing behaviour, introduced you to a model of influences on behaviour. You considered each of them and then ranked them according to the degree of resistance they were creating for your change programme. The action plan you then completed enabled you to make decisions to achieve greater change in behaviour.

Refer to the Change Process Profile on page 15. If appropriate change your score on the profile now that you have completed this section.

Behaviour resistances exercise

Listed below are the eight influences which affect people's behaviour. Read the brief description accompanying each and then mark the influences from 1 to 8 according to the amount of resistance each causes to the objectives of your change programme. Rank as 1 the influence causing the most resistance and rank as 8 the influence causing the least resistance.

Influences	Description	Ranking
Values	The principles on which the organization is based. Are they clear and defined? Are the present organization values consistent with those of the change programme? Do the change champions operate according to the desired values?	
Policy and strategy	The clear statements of the direction the organization is following in its main sphere of operation. Have they been written in an understandable form and communicated to employees? Have the policy and strategy been translated into plans which are now driving the change process?	
Organization structures	The way the organization is structured including the interrelationships of units, departments and functions and the number of job grades and layers of employees. Are the existing structures appropriate for and supportive of the aims of the change programme? Are there any aspects of the organization structure that will inhibit the change process and the required behaviour?	
Organization systems	The numerous systems and procedures which regulate, guide, control and monitor the activities and processes in the organization. Will the existing systems support the change and encourage the new behaviour? Are there any existing systems and procedures that encourage behaviour opposite to that required and which therefore need replacing?	

141

Reproduced from *A Manual for Change*
by Terry Wilson, Gower, Aldershot, 1994.

Organization technology	The technological methods used by the organization to produce its outputs including workplace designs and layouts, computerization and process controls. Is the technology assisting or inhibiting the behaviour required? Are any changes necessary?	
Individual roles	The way that managers' and employees' jobs are structured to enable them to achieve their goals. Are all jobs designed so that people can devote their energies and efforts to implementing the change philosophy? Are people concentrating on the correct objectives? Do the roles enable people to operate with the correct style and behaviour?	
Individual beliefs and attitudes	The beliefs held and the attitudes that employees have to the organization and their work. Will current beliefs and attitudes prevent people behaving according to the philosophy of the change programme? Are some groups of employees more likely to be resistant than others?	
Individual skills	The skills that managers and other employees possess to enable them to behave according to the requirements of the new change philosophy. Are all individuals aware of what is required of them? Are individuals being trained in the new skills?	

Now that you have ranked the influences from 1 to 8, you will be able to see which are creating the greatest resistance to the ultimate goal of changing people's behaviour.

The next stage is to analyse each of the influences in more detail and then plan to overcome them. You can begin this by completing the action plan which starts on page 143.

Behaviour resistance action plan

To complete the action plan start with the influence ranked as 1. This is the one that you consider is creating the greatest resistance to the required behaviour change. Write the influence in the space provided. Consider the influence in detail and identify the main issues that are causing resistance and those that are assisting behaviour change. Write these in the space provided. Now develop an action plan that shows how the resistances can be overcome and the assistance issues reinforced.

Continue this process for all eight influences.

Influence 1 ....

Resistance issues:

Assistance issues:

Action plan:

Reproduced from *A Manual for Change*
by Terry Wilson, Gower, Aldershot, 1994.

Influence 2 ....

Resistance issues:

Assistance issues:

Action plan:

Influence 3 ....

Resistance issues:

Assistance issues:

Action plan:

Influence 4 ....

Resistance issues:

Assistance issues:

Action plan:

Influence 5 ....

Resistance issues:

Assistance issues:

Action plan:

Reproduced from *A Manual for Change*
by Terry Wilson, Gower, Aldershot, 1994.

Influence 6 ....

Resistance issues:

Assistance issues:

Action plan:

Influence 7 ....

Resistance issues:

Assistance issues:

Action plan:

Influence 8 ....

Resistance issues:

Assistance issues:

Action plan:

Factor eleven:
Expertise and resources

Expertise and resources are the food of change

All change programmes require a substantial input of resources and expertise to be implemented successfully. According to the objectives and scale of the programme, there could be changes in almost every aspect of an organization's characteristics from location, buildings, plant, equipment, systems and procedures to philosophy, management style, employment patterns, reward systems, job and role structures and so on. In some change programmes almost nothing is left untouched and many millions of pounds are spent. The management skill lies in understanding which resources are necessary for each aspect of the programme. In addition, at each phase of the programme an assessment has to be made of whether it is necessary to bring in external resources and expertise that is not available within the organization.

This section considers the resources and expertise that will be required to carry out each section of the change process successfully. It concentrates on the resources required to bring about organizational, cultural and management changes. Physical and technological changes are excluded as they vary with the organization's change objectives and are beyond the scope of this manual.

The resources and expertise required for each factor of the change profile are discussed below.

Factor one: Perspectives

Now that you have worked through the various sections of the manual you should know how to maintain an objective view of the change process and how vital this is for success. You will certainly be able to identify the groups of people who will be most and least affected by the change. You will also be aware of those who will perceive themselves as winners and losers and the action that should be taken so that they all perceive themselves as winners. Read and reconsider Factor one. In particular concentrate on the

Perspectives Techniques Survey starting on page 128, examining the methods that you will be using to maintain your perspective and the expertise and resources required.

Factor two: The change champion

You should now be aware of the importance of the change champion to the change programme. Without a champion and a group of disciples, it is unlikely that change will be implemented successfully. The main resource requirements relating to the champion are those which concern time. Throughout the programme the champion will have to maintain a high profile, developing and leading strategy teams and interacting and being known at all levels in the organization. One resource may be a person or group of people who are able to advise and counsel the champion through the many stages of change. There may also be a need for the champion to develop certain attributes to be more effective in the role.

There may be a further need to develop change champion skills in managers further down the organization. This could be achieved through a combination of guidance, coaching and skills training.

Factor three: The nature of change

This factor considers the effects that the nature of the change will have on the organization. The main resources will therefore be required for collecting information or commissioning studies from consultants to enable future scenarios to be developed. This may include visits or research in similar organizations who have responded to the same kinds of changes. An analysis could be made of their response to the change and whether their solutions are applicable to your organization. This information will allow you to identify the actions that are necessary to achieve the change. You will also be more able to assess the likely scope and scale of the programme.

Factor four: Unified management vision

In any significant change programme, particularly those involving a shift in philosophy or management style, the importance of a consistent, unified view cannot be overemphasized. When such changes are taking place, people look to senior managers for signs of the new philosophy happening in practice. Therefore, if teamwork and more open communication are the aims of a programme and only half the senior managers agree with and practise these concepts, the people below them will be confused and unable to believe that the change champions are serious in their intentions. A unified management vision comes about when senior managers agree and understand what the vision means and then behave according to it. This may involve a training and development process for all managers with individual help and guidance being given as the change progresses. All managers must also take personal responsibility for their own actions and realize how they can influence the change process.

150

Factor five: Change of organization philosophy

Changes or shifts in organization philosophy can have a significant effect on people and how they think and act. Quite often it is the intention of the change champion to alter outdated organization values, systems and operating methods substantially. To do this, considerable expertise and resources are necessary. Firstly, the new philosophy has to be explored and developed. It then has to be communicated to the entire organization. People must accept what is being proposed and restructure their roles, jobs and methods of working. At all stages there are teams of people conducting investigations, developing and implementing solutions. Because of the size of the task, additional resources and expertise have to be brought into the organization, either consultants or specialists on short-term contracts.

Factor six: Change phases

Understanding the importance and influence of each change phase is vital. Too often change champions, in their desire for rapid change and results, give too little attention to the 'understanding' and 'accepting' phases. They develop the vision, communicate it and then expect people to behave accordingly. However, before this can happen individuals may have to undergo some traumatic changes in their perceptions and emotions. Values and practices that have guided them for many years have to be discarded and replaced by those which are new and unfamiliar. Therefore far longer than expected may have to be spent on helping people to understand and accept the vision. This will demand resources and communication exercises. An objective outside observer can also be useful to assess the stage that different groups have reached in the change phases. This would help ensure that change initiatives are in line with people's current position. For example, it could be a costly and wasteful exercise to train managers in a more open and consultative style when they have not accepted the need for such a change.

Factor seven: The 10/90 rule

Like the change phases, the 10/90 rule is an important part of the process of change that has to be fully understood and responded to correctly. The level of energy and commitment to change can soon wane and be replaced by apathy and doubt that the programme will ever deliver the benefits promised in the vision. To maintain both energy and commitment, a strategy which is both top down and bottom up is necessary. 'Top down' means that the change champion gives regular updates on the progress of the change programme as it affects the organization and its various parts. 'Bottom up' means that employees are involved in developing their future working environments. Change in these circumstances is something that people have some control over, not something that is done to them. By using this approach during the change programme, people come to regard such methods as normal working practice and the involvement in decision making maintains energy and commitment.

151

In both the top down and bottom up strategies, resources are required not only to plan, develop and run presentations, but also to initiate, lead and maintain the many projects that will be under way.

Factor eight: Transitional management

One of the biggest changes when organizations attempt to modernize and renew themselves occurs in the way that managers manage. Many of the concepts aimed at increasing human motivation require managers to be coaches rather than controllers, developers of people rather than stiflers of initiative, supporters and encouragers rather than demotivators. The new role helps people to be independent and self-managing so that they give to their job the same dedication and enthusiasm that they would give to their favourite pastime or hobby. To understand this management style and to operate in this new mode requires investment in training schemes supported by coaching. The management style will pass through a transitional stage between leadership and teamship, and how this is achieved will vary with the people being managed. The style will have to be tested by managers in practical situations with help and guidance from trainers and other mentors.

Factor nine: Teamwork

If you choose the teamwork route to change and a teamwork philosophy for running the organization, then there will need to be a heavy investment in people to help them to understand and practise the principles of teamwork. The first task will be to design the organization so that it is capable of operating on a teamwork basis. Departments and sections should be arranged around workflows and groups of people formed so that they are able to operate as teams. These teams should be trained using the cascade principle and helped to develop teamwork on a daily basis in their workplace. Team leaders must also be trained in the new skills of leadership and in operating the flexible style that is necessary to change from being a leader and manager to being a team member.

Owing to the important part that teamwork plays in the new philosophy of the organization, it is likely that any teamwork programme will be led by experts in forming, selecting and training teams and their leaders. These may be people from within the organization or external consultants.

Factor ten: Changing behaviour

All change efforts are worthless unless people in the organization act differently. Factor ten considers the way that, as organizations have grown over time, their systems, procedures, roles, structures, attitudes and so on have also developed to encourage, support and reinforce the desired behaviour. In many organizations these influences have been shaping behaviour for years, even decades. When an organization decides to change there is little point in senior managers adopting a value, issuing a decree and expecting people to do things differently. Behaviour patterns are extremely resilient and often resistant to change. The task of changing behaviour therefore requires a perceptive and careful analysis of the desired behaviour and the kind of organizational influences that will support it. In organizations where change initiatives have been less than successful, this has often been because there was no understanding of these influences and therefore no action was taken to modify them. Resources must be allocated within a change programme to examine obstacles to behaviour change. Detailed plans can then be made to remove or modify these obstacles.

Your organization

Having reviewed each factor your task now is to assess the expertise and resources that you require for your change programme. You may also wish to refer to the notes that you made on the Change Process Profile on pages 16–19.

Begin the action plan by reading the instructions on page 154.

Summary

Factor eleven, Expertise and resources, enabled you to consider the expertise and resources necessary for implementing your change programme. You identified the type of resources required and whether these were available inside your organization or had to be provided from outside.

Refer to the Change Process Profile on page 15. Now that you have considered the resources required for each factor, examine your score on the profile and adjust it if necessary.

Expertise and resources action plan

Completing the action plan

This action plan is based on an analysis of the resources required to implement each of the factors in the manual. It has three areas: the initiatives and actions that should be taken; the expertise, skills and resources available within the organization; and the expertise, skills and resources that must be brought in from outside the organization. Assess each area and then complete the three columns.

Perspectives	Expertise, skills and resources required	
Main initiatives	Available inside the organization	To be brought into the organization

The change champion	Expertise, skills and resources required	
Main initiatives	**Available inside the organization**	**To be brought into the organization**

The nature of change	Expertise, skills and resources required	
Main initiatives	**Available inside the organization**	**To be brought into the organization**

Reproduced from *A Manual for Change*
by Terry Wilson, Gower, Aldershot, 1994.

Unified management vision	Expertise, skills and resources required	
Main initiatives	Available inside the organization	To be brought into the organization

Change of organization philosophy	Expertise, skills and resources required	
Main initiatives	Available inside the organization	To be brought into the organization

Change phases	Expertise, skills and resources required	
Main initiatives	Available inside the organization	To be brought into the organization

The 10/90 rule	Expertise, skills and resources required	
Main initiatives	Available inside the organization	To be brought into the organization

Transitional management	Expertise, skills and resources required	
Main initiatives	Available inside the organization	To be brought into the organization

Teamwork	Expertise, skills and resources required	
Main initiatives	Available inside the organization	To be brought into the organization

Reproduced from *A Manual for Change*
by Terry Wilson, Gower, Aldershot, 1994.

Changing behaviour	Expertise, skills and resources required	
Main initiatives	Available inside the organization	To be brought into the organization

After conducting this review you now have a much clearer idea of the expertise and resources that will be required to implement your change programme. It is, however, only an overview and a great deal more thought and planning will have to take place for each area of your programme.

Factor twelve:
Dangers and pitfalls

Change without pain only exists in the minds of the naive

It may seem paradoxical to include this section when radical change is about hope, confidence, a brighter future, new opportunities and benefits to the organization and its employees. Indeed, many change programmes do have these results but they do not arise automatically. The process of achieving them is frequently difficult and tortuous, with many dangers and obstacles to be overcome.

One often reads case histories of change programmes that are beacons of perfection and achievement. Objectives have been set, pursued and successfully implemented. All actions and interventions appear to have been successful and now most of the organization's employees are fully supportive of the changes and working together to build the future. It is unfortunate that similar attention is not given in these case histories to the many difficulties encountered, since solving problems often produces the real successes and turning-points of a change programme.

Every organization change programme has characteristics that make it unique. These may relate to trading circumstances, management style, financial constraints, products, markets, technology, trade union activity and so on. The change strategy adopted will be designed to accommodate any relevant considerations and be flexible enough to handle any others which arise during the change process.

There are a number of dangers that face organization change programmes, some of which are described below.

Plunging in too deeply

Some change programmes are part of an organization's planned strategic development. In many other organizations, however, change results from the realization that without significant business reappraisal, refurbishment and modernization, the future trading position of the business will be in jeopardy. This realization leads to an analysis of all aspects of the business

161

which enables the change champions to assess how far behind current practice they are in technology, organization and business philosophies, how their position relates to that of their competitors, and so on. They then have to decide how deeply they plunge into the organization refurbishment programme. Do they tackle all the issues at once or deal with them gradually over a period of several years? Furthermore, do they adopt only tried and tested ideas and technology or become pioneers and develop new thinking, techniques and processes? The first strategy would bring them level with their most successful competitors, the second would place them ahead of all others in their field.

Before this decision is made, the change champions visit known centres of excellence, consultants, experts, plant and equipment manufacturers and so on to determine exactly what is accepted modern practice. They will then be in a position to assess the degree of risk involved in adopting new ideas, philosophies, systems, procedures, computers or plant and equipment and can decide what should be introduced into their organization.

One of the dangers to be avoided is plunging in too deeply and adopting a system or philosphy that has not been fully tested. It is easy to see why this decision would be made in the atmosphere of hope, expectation and sometimes euphoria which pervades the vision building phase. However, many change programmes have been delayed for a considerable time by equipment that would not perform to the expected standard. Expensive development work and modifications have to take place which are disruptive to the organization and sometimes place the change champion in a vulnerable position. Similarly, the change champions may be attempting to negotiate new working practices to which employees and trade unions are opposed. Until this point the champion has been sustained by visions and expectations, but now is the time to deliver palpable results and they are not forthcoming. More senior managers and people from head office start to take a closer interest in the process. After a time if there has been insufficient progress a new change champion could be recruited whose job would be to renegotiate targets and give new thinking and direction to the change programme.

Change champions must not get too carried away with visions and idealism. These are part of the change process, but they must be tempered by commercial business realities. If change champions do plunge in too deeply and are unable to deliver business objectives on time, they will suffer the inevitable consequences.

Trade union opposition

The stance that the trade unions take can have a significant effect on the timescale and progress of the change programme. Many programmes propose radical changes to the relationships between management, trade unions and the people they represent, such as single table bargaining where all the different unions negotiate with management collectively rather than separately. Agreements based on general principles replace the plethora of custom and practice agreements and negotiated procedures which have governed management/union activities for many years. Staff status and equal conditions may be proposed for all categories of employee.

Flexibility and a multi-skilled workforce may be aims of the change champions. In some programmes the list of changes can appear endless and may affect the beliefs and practices that are fundamental for many union officials and shop stewards.

Another complication which arises is that frequently radical change involves shedding employees, either through voluntary or compulsory redundancy. It is then easy for a psychological battle to take place between the change champions and the trade union representatives based on job shedding versus job preservation. Both managers and unions realize that people represent a significant cost in any organization, therefore if the business could be run with fewer employees this would make a large contribution to achieving the commercial and financial targets of the change programme. Unions usually take a defensive stance, giving little co-operation and support to the programme and only conceding changes when they have no other choice. In some instances unions withdraw completely from any dialogue or co-operation and only become involved when they can negotiate over proposals from management.

Change programmes often propose a new role for trade union representatives, moving from one based predominantly on negotiation to one involving far more joint problem solving and joint decision making, from confrontation to co-operation and partnership. This can cause difficulties on both sides. People may be uneasy with the new roles and relationships. Suspicion and mistrust may be carried over from the old relationships and be difficult to overcome. Furthermore, it is possible that a real partnership may never be offered by management. The most important decisions affecting the organization will still be taken by senior managers and the unions will then be asked to agree and recommend them to their members. Union involvement in decision making is confined to peripheral issues such as health and safety, car parking, work clothes and so on.

Apart from the problems of attitude that union representatives may have when they are asked to perform a problem-solving and decision-making role, there may also be a lack of skill which is frequently overlooked. Many organizational problems are complex. They demand special skills, knowledge and insights which managers have spent many years acquiring. Union representatives will probably not have invested time in this way and they often do not possess the same perception and understanding as managers. This puts them at a disadvantage when they are asked to solve wide-ranging organizational problems. They tend to think about detail and also about how any actions would affect their members on a day-to-day basis.

Another obstacle encountered by some trade union representatives, like some managers, is that they have difficulty coming to grips with the faith and vision of the change champions. Their job and day-to-day existence are practical and pragmatic and can be understood. They have not experienced the vision being promised by the change champion. It is therefore easy to reject the vision of how things can be and remain with what they know.

Trade union opposition may also arise owing to the transient nature of senior managers. Many trade union representatives have been with the organization for some years and have seen several change champions come and go. They question whether the change will actually happen. Is this an initiative that will reach fruition, or will the change champion move on and

163

be replaced by another who will take the organization in a different direction? This kind of thinking can result in resistance and a lack of commitment to the change programme, particularly in its early stages.

Short-term and long-term objectives

Most change programmes, particularly if they involve a change of management philosophy, have to try to satisfy two sets of objectives, which may be in conflict. The first objectives concern producing the goods, services and outputs to satisfy existing customers. The second objectives are to do with introducing the change and new methods of managing and operating which will be the basis of the future organization.

This second set of objectives may involve a culture change, elements of which may be directly opposed to the present operating methods. The management style might, for example, have to change from directing and controlling to teamwork and consensus. This change will take time and during that period senior managers and the rest of the organization will have to be tolerant of mistakes and a possible decrease in output. Owing to the commercial day-to-day pressures placed on managers by customers and senior managers, there is a danger that they will revert to an autocratic style in an attempt to satisfy the short-term objectives. Such a behaviour change may produce the desired outputs but it will leave people confused and doubting the change champions' sincerity.

This kind of conflict can also arise in the area of service or product quality. When there is pressure to achieve targets and maintain output, it is easy to forget the new philosophy of quality and excellence and give the customers substandard service in order to satisfy output requirements.

Managers should be aware of the potential conflicts between short-term and long-term aims and be able to manage both effectively. The organization has to operate and satisfy its external customers while at the same time developing itself for the future.

The vulnerability of the change champion

Managers initiating and leading an organizational change programme find themselves at risk of being replaced, offered alternative employment or dismissed if the programme runs into difficulties or fails to produce the stated benefits on time. On the other hand, if the programme is successful and recognized as radical and innovative by the business community, then accolades will be awarded. The change champion may receive rapid promotion or be asked to write books and articles, address prestigious conferences, make documentary films or be a consultant on similar programmes. In addition, there will also be numerous visits from managers of other organizations who are seeking detailed information about the programme and how it was implemented.

There are many reasons for a programme not achieving its objectives and it is likely that at least some success will be achieved. Radical change programmes comprise numerous individual projects involving many facets of the business. These projects could concern new buildings, plant and equipment, new products, different organization structures, additional or more complex computer control systems, new methods of motivating and rewarding people and so on. Many of these individual projects will be successful but the programme as a whole will be judged on how effectively it produces the desired outputs and the way in which they are achieved.

Many businesses are part of larger organizations and there has to be understanding and empathy between the separate parts of the larger organization. No matter how innovative and radical the change champions may wish to be, they have to be aware of the necessary relationships with the wider organization. Redesigning payment systems so that a free flow of managers across the organization is not possible would not be welcomed. Neither would the introduction of one-off, specialist systems which disrupt the centralized systems operating in head office. The final design has to fit in with the wider environment in which the organization has to operate.

Change champions must realize that they are often taking substantial risks with their organizations and their own careers. They must also be prepared to accept the consequences if the programme fails.

Change of champion

In some circumstances the change champion leading the programme may be replaced. The effect of this replacement on the direction of the programme will depend on why it happened. Some programmes gradually run into trouble, falling further and further behind in their output targets either because of technical problems, resistance from the people involved or faulty design. Owing to these problems the change champion may be replaced, which can have a significant effect on the programme and the direction it then takes. The new champion is brought in as a saviour. He or she may have no responsibility for, or commitment to, the previous programme and is therefore able to make radical changes by renegotiating key parameters and outputs. In doing this, resources may be increased, timescales changed or personnel replaced. This gives the programme a second chance, with a corresponding increase in commitment from those involved as more realistic targets are set.

Another result of a change of champion can be a shift in management style and philosophy. The change of style which may be part of the programme is determined by the change champion's values and beliefs. A new champion with different beliefs may overturn some of the previous ideas. The open-plan offices constructed by the first champion, for example, could be replaced by individual offices and partitions. A management style of consensus and openness may slowly be changed to one of individual targets and control. Perspectives and initiatives designed to develop the long-term culture of the organization may be abandoned to satisfy immediate commercial needs. The new champion has been brought in to put the programme on course and to show that this is happening concentrates on areas which will show an immediate return.

There may also be a change of champion as part of the natural development of the change process. The initial stages of some programmes require a strong, powerful and resolute champion who is able to break down resistances and overcome obstacles. Discussion, debate and mutual decision making may be the aims of a new culture, but if managers are unable to take decisions sufficiently quickly then the change champion will decide on their behalf. The champion energizes the organization and takes the programme through its early stages. Battles are fought and won with some casualties along the way. After a time it is necessary to have a different style of change champion and leadership, one that concentrates on building trust, cohesiveness and harmony and that develops the new culture. At this point, the change champion may be replaced by a softer, more consensus-seeking leader whose objective is to consolidate the new management philosophy and to help people to operate in the new way.

Shortage of resources

Organizations usually only embark on change programmes when they have sufficient financial resources to carry them out. Programmes involving a significant shift in culture are unlikely to be begun in an organization that is struggling for survival and in which there is an acute shortage of resources and a necessity for compulsory redundancies. Significant change may nevertheless occur in how work in this organization is accomplished, but it is likely to be the result of the employees' fear of losing their jobs. This kind of change will incur a cost in terms of understanding, commitment and employees' longer-term motivation.

Consensus change programmes operate on a different financial basis. Budgets are allocated to some of the 'softer' aspects such as training, team development, harmonization schemes or communications exercises. These set the correct tone for the programme and develop the new skills necessary to run the organization. However, if resources become scarce then the whole initiative may be abandoned. For example, the leadership and team-building programme that all managers are to attend to enable them to understand and develop their new style is cancelled owing to lack of capital. However, other change projects involving new plant and equipment are spared since hardware is perceived to be more capable of contributing to the aims of the programme.

During a programme that will take several years to complete, there is always the danger that resources will be cut if there is a shortage of cash. If this shortage is acute, then only hardware projects will proceed and little will be done to change the management philosophy and style.

Work climate

Change programmes create significant pressures for the change champions, other managers and key members of the workforce. They are asked to do two jobs: maintain the output and productivity of the organization at its present level to satisfy customers, and at the same time build the organization of the future. Furthermore when developing the future organization they are frequently dealing with unknown and unfamiliar areas, more difficult for most people to accommodate than those which are known and familiar.

Many people connected with the change process will work long hours.

The change champion and managers will have frequent project meetings and impromptu encounters with a variety of people, from consultants, technical experts and trade union representatives, to craftspeople, contractors and supervisors. There will also be increased pressure from senior managers to achieve not only the day-to-day outputs of the organization, but also the targets of the change programme.

The work climate will be one of constant activity, pace and an emphasis on results. To survive, people will have to be flexible, deal with uncertainty, cope with pressure and possess resolve and stamina. However, not everyone is capable of coping with such a set of circumstances for a prolonged period. If people are not affected physically or mentally, their judgement and work output may suffer owing to overwork and fatigue.

It is therefore important for the change champions to monitor the work climate during each stage of the programme and take any steps necessary to prevent breakdown or loss of efficiency through overwork.

Inadequate understanding

When an organization decides to embark on a change programme it is frequently attracted to current management concepts which it wants to incorporate into its new philosophy. Often these can be apparently simple ideas such as teamwork, consensus decision making, an enterprise culture, total quality management or excellence. All forward-looking managers would espouse such ideas and want to build them into their organization. The danger is that an organization may adopt these ideas without fully understanding what they are, what they mean and how they can be built into the organization.

For example, adopting an enterprise culture has significant implications for the style of the organization and how it is run and managed. Firstly, enterprise has to be defined and understood by the change champions. In addition, the kind of behaviour that is required of all people in the organization when they are being enterprising has to be identified. There should be a clear definition of the outcomes of enterprising behaviour and the benefits that will be gained. A third area to be addressed is how enterprise is to be managed in the organization. For large organizations this can pose a dilemma since enterprise is about giving people freedom and empowering them to make decisions and use their creativity. At the same time the organization still needs to regulate and control work. Unless managed correctly, these two can be in conflict. The final area to be considered is how enterprise can be started and encouraged to grow and develop in an organization. This would involve management initiatives, training programmes and systems for rewarding enterprising behaviour.

Another example of a popular concept is customer care. Many organizations have their customer charters prominently displayed and while the service offered by some businesses has been transformed, such charters have had little effect on others. This is because the managers have never fully understood customer service and the actions that have to be taken to introduce and sustain it.

External expertise

Change programmes are in essence concerned with modernizing and revitalizing an organization. All organizations are in danger of expending most of their energy on producing familiar outputs or making profits while change and innovation in the wider environment go unnoticed. The organization then falls behind its competitors in its operating methods, philosophies and outputs. Once this decline reaches a certain level, change champions emerge to offer salvation and a new future. The foundation of this new future is new ideas, which are often found outside the organization. There are many agencies whose main purpose is to create, develop and introduce new ideas into organizations. These include consultancies, universities, research institutions, machine manufacturers and government departments. The changing organization must spend adequate time looking for, considering and evaluating all potential new ideas to help with the renewal process.

Outside agencies therefore offer ideas, techniques and systems with which the new organization can be built. They also have experience of implementing their ideas and will have found solutions to many of the problems, which will save the organization considerable time and effort. There are obviously some areas where the organization may feel that it does possess the expertise and experience necessary to handle a specific project, and in this case no outside help will be required.

Outside expertise, although sometimes expensive, does offer the changing organization the benefit of objectivity. Change champions and project teams can frequently be so close to a situation that they overlook or misinterpret certain information. This is because their thinking is constrained by their experience in the organization. An outside person with different knowledge and experience may interpret situations more objectively and hence save valuable time and resources in implementing solutions.

One of the dangers of using external resources is that they may sell products and services that are inappropriate. External agencies, contractors and consultancies are also subject to commercial aims and pressures in the same way as any organization. Change champions should evaluate carefully any products or services offered by external agencies to ensure that they will produce the required benefits.

In summary, external expertise therefore offers many of the new ideas according to which the future organization will be designed. A radical change programme is unlikely to be successful without the use of external agencies to introduce new ideas, thinking and ways of running the business. However, external agencies do have to be carefully evaluated to ensure that what they offer is suitable for the developing organization.

Your organization

Having read about some of the dangers and pitfalls that can affect a change programme, now assess your own programme. This is done by completing the D and P Profile which starts on page 170. Please follow the instructions. You should also review the notes that you made on the Change Process Profile on pages 16–19.

Summary

Factor twelve, Dangers and pitfalls, helped you to consider issues that could be detrimental to your change programme. You assessed the influence of the issues and identified the six most important. Finally you decided on the actions that needed to be taken.

Refer to the Change Process Profile on page 15. If necessary adjust your score based on your additional analysis.

D and P profile

Completing the profile

How you complete the profile will depend on the state of your change programme. If you are about to start a programme, complete the profile based on your assessment of the potential dangers and pitfalls. Alternatively, you may be some way through your programme and already experiencing some dangers and pitfalls.

To complete the profile, assess the percentage probability of each issue adversely affecting the change process. For example, if you think that you are 'plunging in too deeply' (PITD) in certain areas in the programme, then assess the percentage probability of adverse effects. At this stage do not try to be too specific, limit your assessment to your own knowledge. If you think that in certain areas in the programme you are plunging in far too deeply and the effect of this will be significant, perhaps even to the extent of jeopardizing the whole project, then allocate a high score, even 100%. If you feel that you are taking almost no risks and not plunging in, then allocate a low score, possibly 0%. If you think that you are taking some risks, score as appropriate between 0% and 100%. Indicate the percentage risk by drawing a line across the PITD column on the profile. Follow the same process for all the other issues.

In the additional columns provided on the profile, add any other issues not covered but which you see as relevant to your particular programme.

D and P profile

PITD — Plunging in too deeply
TUO — Trade union opposition
SLTO — Short- and long-term objectives
CCV — Change champion vulnerability
COC — Change of champion

SOR — Shortage of resources
WC — Work climate
IU — Inadequate understanding
EE — External expertise

Percentage adverse effect on programme

	100
	90
	80
	70
	60
	50
	40
	30
	20
	10
	0

PITD	TUO	SLTO	CCV	COC	SOR	WC	IU	EE

D and P issues

171
Reproduced from *A Manual for Change*
by Terry Wilson, Gower, Aldershot, 1994.

D and P Action planning

Now that you have identified the issues that are adversely affecting the change programme or have potential adverse effects, the next stage is to analyse the six most important issues and then plan action to eradicate them.

Concentrate first on the issue on which your score was highest. If you scored 100% on one issue, then clearly this is the first priority. Analyse the other five issues in descending order of priority.

Write the name of the issue and the percentage score that you allocated it in the box below. Determine and write down the reasons for your scores. When you are clear about the reasons, detail the action to be taken to correct the problem.

Issue 1 .... **% score** ....
Reasons for score:
Actions to be taken:

Reproduced from *A Manual for Change*
by Terry Wilson, Gower, Aldershot, 1994.

Issue 2.. **% score**....................................

Reasons for score:

Actions to be taken:

Issue 3.. **% score**....................................

Reasons for score:

Actions to be taken:

Reproduced from *A Manual for Change*
by Terry Wilson, Gower, Aldershot, 1994.

Issue 4.. **% score**....................................

Reasons for score:

Actions to be taken:

Issue 5.. **% score**..................................

Reasons for score:

Actions to be taken:

Reproduced from *A Manual for Change*
by Terry Wilson, Gower, Aldershot, 1994.

Issue 6 .... **% score** ....
Reasons for score:
Actions to be taken:

This analysis should have given you valuable insights into your change programme, irrespective of whether you are just starting, part of the way through or nearly completed. Reflect on the actions that you propose to take and decide your next moves.